Evolutionary Optimization: the μGP toolkit

Ernesto Sanchez • Massimiliano Schillaci
Giovanni Squillero

Evolutionary Optimization: the µGP toolkit

Springer

Ernesto Sanchez
Politecnico di Torino
Dipto. Automatica e Informatica
Corso Duca degli Abruzzi 24
10129 Torino
Italy
ernesto.sanchez@polito.it

Giovanni Squillero
Politecnico di Torino
Dipto. Automatica e Informatica
Corso Duca degli Abruzzi 24
10129 Torino
Italy
giovanni.squillero@polito.it

Massimiliano Schillaci
ICT Consultant
massimiliano.schillaci@gmail.com

ISBN 978-1-4899-9368-7   ISBN 978-0-387-09426-7 (eBook)
DOI 10.1007/978-0-387-09426-7
Springer New York Dordrecht Heidelberg London

© Springer Science+Business Media, LLC 2011
Softcover re-print of the Hardcover 1st edition 2011

Printed on acid-free paper

Springer is part of Springer Science+Business Media (www.springer.com)

A life spent making mistakes is not only more honorable, but more useful than a life spent doing nothing.

George Bernard Shaw

Preface

μGP is a computational approach for autonomously pursuing a goal defined by the user. To this end, candidate solutions for the given task are repeatedly modified, evaluated and enhanced. The alteration process mimics some principles of the Neo-Darwinian paradigm, such as *variation, inheritance*, and *selection*. μGP has been developed in *Politecnico di Torino* since 2000. Its original application was the generation of assembly-language programs for different types of microprocessors, hence the Greek letter *micro* in the name. Its name is sometimes spelled *MicroGP* or uGP due to typographic limitations. μGP is free software: it can be redistributed and modified under the terms of the GNU General Public License[1].

μGP is ordinarily utilized to find the optimal solution of hard problems, and it has been demonstrated able to outperform both human experts and conventional heuristics in such a task. In order to exploit the approach, the user describes the *appearance* of the solutions to his problem and provides a program able to evaluate them. The tool implementing the approach fosters a set of random solutions, and iteratively refines them in discrete steps. Its heuristic local-search algorithm uses the result of the evaluations, together with other internal information, to focus on the regions of the search space that look more promising, and eventually to produce an optimal solution.

μGP is an *evolutionary algorithm*. Different candidate solutions are considered in each step of the search process, and new ones are generated through mechanisms that ape both sexual and asexual reproduction. New solutions *inherit* distinctive traits from existing ones, and may coalesce the good characteristics of different *parents*. Better solutions have a greater chance to reproduce, and to succeed in the simulated struggle for existence.

Candidate solutions are internally encoded as graphs, or, more precisely, as directed multigraphs[2]. During the search process, multigraphs are constrained by a user-defined set of rules to conform to sensible structures. They are transformed

---

[1] For more information, and how to apply and follow the GNU GPL, see http://www.gnu.org/licenses/

[2] A directed multigraph is a graph where a direction is assigned to each edge, and the same pair of vertices may be joined by more than one edge

to text files according to user-defined rules, and fed to a user-defined evaluation program. Thus, no knowledge about the problem being solved is included in μGP itself.

For an industry practitioner, μGP is a versatile optimizer able to tackle almost any problem with a limited setup effort. All the configuration is contained in XML[3] files, that can be created with simple text editors or powerful ad-hoc tools. μGP routinely handles problems that require solutions in the form of full-fledged assembly programs, including functions, interrupt handlers and data. But a much wider range of different problems can be tackled, including optimization of mathematical functions represented as trees, integer and combinatorial optimization, and real value optimization. While μGP is theoretically able to work with a problem that requires a simple unstructured solution, it may not be the best option in such cases, except, perhaps, for the easiness of set up. On the contrary, it should be exploited on tasks that involve the concurrent optimization of different data types, and when solutions exhibit quite complex structures.

This book shows how to effectively use μGP to solve an industrial problem. For this purpose, the text assumes that the user is competent in the application domain, but requires only a basic understanding of information technology. Moreover, only limited knowledge of the evolutionary computation field is required. The practitioner is guided through a list of easy steps to complete the setup. Moreover, an extensive discussion on the meaning and effect of the various parameters that can be tuned to increase the overall performance is provided.

For an evolutionary computation scholar, μGP may be regarded as a platform where new operators and strategies can be easily tested. Additionally, it presents some features that may be considered of interest: the possibility to shape the behavior smoothly from steady-state to generational, including several degrees of elitism; self adaptation of operator strength, operator activation probability, tournament size, population size and number of applied operators; diversity protection, trough population entropy and delta-entropy of individuals; fitness holes; clone detection, with optional scaling or extermination; support for different population topologies, from panmictic to lattice; multiple populations, including support for migrations; support for dynamic fitness functions; support for parallel fitness evaluation; multiple fitness, either priority-based or multi-objective.

Considering this latter goal, the book details the conceptual architecture and the implementation of the tool. While the text aims at self-containment, a basic knowledge of the evolutionary computation theory may be useful. Indeed, to fully understand the implementation details, a good knowledge of the C++ language is also required.

The book is organized in several broad sections. Chapters 1 and 2 introduce the reader to the field of evolutionary computation and provide a rationale for the whole book. Chapters 3 and 4 outline the main features of μGP from a theoretical point of

---

[3] XML stands for *extensible markup language*. It was developed by the World Wide Web Consortium (W3C) in the late 1990s, and defines a set of rules for encoding generic documents electronically.

view. Chapter 5 introduces the complete work flow for using μGP, and may provide a quick start for the impatient reader. Chapters 6, 7, 8, 9 and 10 cover the gory details of configuring the tool, running it and tweaking its many parameters. Chapter 11 illustrates the details of the μGP architecture and its implementation. Chapter 12 provides several examples of use of the tool, showing both the effect of tuning the evolution parameters, and several possible ways to approach problems to which the tool does not seem directly applicable. Finally, a couple of appendixes list all the possible options, parameters and special values that the tool recognizes inside its configuration files, together with a brief explanation of their use.

We would like to acknowledge some colleagues and friends who helped us in this project over the past ten years: Alessandro Aimo, Antonio Casaschi, Paolo Bernardi, Fulvio Corno, Gianluca Cumani, Davide Decicco, Sonia Drappero, Paolo Ferretti, Michelangelo Grosso, Germán Labarga, William Lindsay, Marco Loggia, Giuseppe Macchia, Onofrio Mancuso, Luca Motta, Zul Nazdri, Danilo Ravotto, Tommaso Rosato, Alessandro Salomone, Fabio Salto, Matteo Sonza Reorda, Luca Sterpone, Antonio Tomasiello, Giuseppe Trovato, Pier Paolo Ucchino, Massimo Violante, Gianluca Zaniolo.

We must dedicate a special thank to Alberto Tonda, who spent his Ph.D. enhancing and tweaking μGP. This book would not have been possible without his work and passion.

Torino,   *Ernesto Sanchez*
Winter 2010   *Massimiliano Schillaci*
                                                                  Giovanni Squillero

Contents

1   Evolutionary computation 1
  1.1   Natural and artificial evolution............................. 1
  1.2   The classical paradigms 4
  1.3   Genetic programming 7

2   Why yet another one evolutionary optimizer? 9
  2.1   Background 9
  2.2   Where to draw the lines 10
  2.3   Individuals 11
  2.4   Problem specification 13
  2.5   Coding Techniques 14

3   The μGP architecture 17
  3.1   Conceptual design 18
  3.2   The evolutionary core 18
        3.2.1   Evolutionary Operators 19
        3.2.2   Population 20
  3.3   The Evolutionary Cycle 21
        3.3.1   Genetic operator selection 21
        3.3.2   Parents selection 22
        3.3.3   Offspring Generation 23
        3.3.4   Individual Evaluation and Slaughtering 24
        3.3.5   Termination and Aging 24

4   Advanced features 27
  4.1   Self adaptation for exploration or exploitation 27
        4.1.1   Self-adaptation inertia 28
        4.1.2   Operator strength 28
        4.1.3   Tournament size 29
  4.2   Escaping local optimums 29
        4.2.1   Operator activation probability 30

        4.2.2   Tuning the elitism.................................... 30
  4.3   Preserving diversity... 31
        4.3.1   Clone detection, scaling and extermination 32
        4.3.2   Entropy and delta-entropy computation 32
        4.3.3   Fitness holes 33
        4.3.4   Population topology and multiple populations 34
  4.4   Coping with the real problems............................... 35
        4.4.1   Parallel fitness evaluation 36
        4.4.2   Multiple fitness 37

5   Performing an evolutionary run 39
  5.1   Robot Pathfinder 41
  5.2 μGP Settings 43
  5.3   Population Settings 45
  5.4   Library of Constraints..................................... 49
  5.5   Launching the experiment 53
  5.6 μGP Extractor 55

6   Command line syntax 57
  6.1   Starting a run 57
  6.2   Controlling messages to the user 58
  6.3   Getting help and information 59
  6.4   Controlling logging....................................... 59
  6.5   Controlling recovery 60
  6.6   Controlling evolution 61
  6.7   Controlling evaluation 62

7   Syntax of the settings file 65
  7.1   Controlling evolution 66
  7.2   Controlling logging....................................... 68
  7.3   Controlling recovery 69

8   Syntax of the population parameters file 71
  8.1   Strategy parameters....................................... 71
        8.1.1   Base parameters 72
        8.1.2   Parameters for self adaptation 75
        8.1.3   Other parameters 78

9   Syntax of the external constraints file 81
  9.1   Purposes of the constraints................................ 81
  9.2   Organization of constraints and hierarchy 82
  9.3   Specifying the structure of the individual 87
  9.4   Specifying the contents of the individual 90

10 Writing a compliant evaluator 97
    10.1 Information from μGP to the fitness evaluator 97
    10.2 Expected fitness format 98
        10.2.1 Good Examples 99
        10.2.2 Bad Examples 100

11 Implementation details 103
    11.1 Design principles 103
    11.2 Architectural choices 104
        11.2.1 The Graph library 105
        11.2.2 The Evolutionary Core library 107
        11.2.3 Front end 114
    11.3 Code organization and class model 114

12 Examples and applications 125
    12.1 Classical one-max 125
        12.1.1 Fitness evaluator 126
        12.1.2 Constraints 128
        12.1.3 Population settings 130
        12.1.4 μGP settings 132
        12.1.5 Running 133
    12.2 Values of parameters and their influence on the evolution:
         Arithmetic expressions 134
        12.2.1 De Jong 3 134
        12.2.2 De Jong 4 - Modified 139
        12.2.3 Carrom 140
    12.3 Complex individuals' structures and evaluation:
         Bit-counting in Assembly 146
        12.3.1 Assembly individuals representation 146
        12.3.2 Evaluator 149
        12.3.3 Running 151

Argument and option synopsis 153

External constraints synopsis 169

References 177

Chapter 1
Evolutionary computation

It always is advisable to perceive clearly our ignorance.

Charles Robert Darwin

Evolution is the theory postulating that all the various types of living organisms have their origin in other preexisting types, and that the differences are due to modifications inherited through successive generations. *Evolutionary computation* is the offshoot of computer science focusing on algorithms inspired by the theory of evolution. The definition is deliberately vague since the boundaries of the field are not, and cannot be, defined clearly. Evolutionary computation is a branch of *computational intelligence*, and it is included into the broad framework of *bio-inspired heuristics*. We shall distinguish explicitly between *natural evolution* and *artificial evolution* to avoid confusion whenever necessary.

This chapter sketches the basics of evolutionary computation and introduces its terminology. A comprehensive compendium of the field is out of the scope of this book, and most concepts are defined only to the extent they are required in what follows. Interested readers will find several fascinating books on the topic, such as [6]. Moreover, a survey of evolutionary theories is beyond our knowledge. We can only suggest [5] and [12] as starting points into the vast and fascinating world of biology.

1.1 Natural and artificial evolution

Natural evolution is a cornerstone of modern biology, and scientists show a remarkable consensus on the topic. The original theories of *evolution* and *natural selection* proposed almost concurrently and independently by Charles Robert Darwin [4] and Alfred Russel Wallace [21] in 19th century, combined with *selectionism* by Charles Weismann [23] and genetics by Gregor Mendel [22], are accepted ubiquitously in the scientific community, as well as widespread among the general public. This coherent corpus, often named *Neo-Darwinism*, acts as a *grand unifying theory* for biology: it is able to explain the wonders of life, and, most noticeably, it does it starting from a limited number of relatively simple and intuitively plausible concepts. It describes the whole process of evolution through notions such as *reproduction, vari-*

ation, competition, and *selection*. Reproduction is the process of generating an off-spring from parents where the progeny inherit traits of their predecessors. Variation is the unexpected alteration of a trait. Competition and selection are the inevitable results of the strive for survival caused by an environment with limited resources.

Evolution can be easily described as a sequence of steps, some mostly deterministic and some mostly random [15]. Such an idea of random forces shaped by deterministic pressures is inspiring and, not surprisingly, has been exploited to describe phenomena quite unrelated to biology. Notable examples include alternatives conceived during learning [3], ideas striving to survive in our culture [5], or even possible universes [24] [18].

Evolution may be seen as an improving process that perfect raw features. Indeed, this is a mistake that eminent biologists like Richard Dawkins and Stephen Jay Gould warn us not to do. Nevertheless, if evolution is seen as a force pushing toward a goal, another terrible misunderstanding, it must be granted that it worked quite well: in some billion years, it turned unorganized cells into wings, eyes, and other amazingly complex structures without requiring any *a priori* design. The whole neo-Darwinist paradigm may thus be regarded as a powerful optimization tool able to produce great results starting from scratch, not requiring a plan, and exploiting a mix of random and deterministic operators.

Dismissing biologists' complaints, evolutionary computation practitioners loosely mimic the natural process to solve their problems. Since they do not know how their goal could be reached, at least not in details, they exploit some neo-Darwinian principles to cultivate sets of solutions in artificial environments, iteratively modifying them in discrete steps. The problem indirectly defines the environment where solutions strive for survival. The process has a defined goal. The simulated evolution is simplistic, when not even implausible. Notwithstanding, successes are routinely reported in the scientific literature. Solutions in a given step inherit qualifying traits from solutions in the previous ones, and optimal results emerge from the artificial primeval soup.

In evolutionary computation, a single candidate solution is termed *individual*; the set of all candidate solutions that exists at a particular time is called *population*, and each step of the evolution process a *generation*. The ability of an individual to solve the given problem is measured by the *fitness function*, which ranks how likely one solution is to propagate its characteristics to the next generations. Most of the jargon of evolutionary computation mimics the precise terminology of biology. The word *genome* denotes the whole genetic material of the organism, although its actual implementation differs from one approach to another. The *gene* is the functional unit of inheritance, or, operatively, the smallest fragment of the genome that may be modified during the evolution process. Genes are positioned in the genome at specific positions called *loci*, the plural of *locus*. The alternative genes that may occur at a given locus are called *alleles*.

The natural processes that lead to mutations, reproduction, competition and selection are emulated by *operators*. Operators act on genes, single individuals, groups or entire populations, usually producing a modified version of the entity they manipulate.

Biologists need to distinguish between the *genotype* and the *phenotype*: the former is all the genetic constitution of an organism; the latter is the set of observable properties that are produced by the interaction between the genotype and the environment. In many implementations, evolutionary computation practitioners do not require such a precise distinction. The numerical value representing the fitness of an individual is sometimes assimilated to its phenotype.

To generate the offspring for the next generation, most evolutionary algorithms implement sexual and asexual reproduction. The former is usually named *recombination*; it necessitates two or more participants, and implies the possibility for the offspring to inherit different characteristics from different parents. When recombination is achieved through a simple exchange of genetic material between the parents, it often takes the name of *crossover*. The latter is named *replication*, to indicate that a copy of an individual is created, or, more commonly, *mutation*, to stress that the copy is not exact. Almost no evolutionary algorithm takes gender into account; hence, individuals do not have distinct reproductive roles. In some implementations, mutation takes place only after the sexual recombination. Noticeably, some evolutionary algorithms do not store a collection of distinct individuals, and therefore reproduction is performed modifying the statistical parameters that describe the current population. All operators exploited during reproduction can be cumulatively called *evolutionary operators*, or *genetic operators* stressing that they act at the genotypical level.

Mutation and recombination introduce variability in the population. *Parent selection* is also usually a stochastic process, albeit biased by the fitness. The population broadens and contracts rhythmically at each generation. First, it widens when the offspring are generated. Then, it shrinks when individuals are discarded. The deterministic step usually involves deciding which individuals are chosen for survival from one generation to the next. This step may be called *survivor selection*, or just *selection*.

Evolutionary algorithms may be defined local search algorithms since they sample a region of the search space dependent upon their actual state, and the offspring loosely define the concept of neighborhood. Since they are based on the trial and error paradigm, they are heuristic algorithms. They are not usually able to mathematically guarantee an optimal solution in a finite time, whereas interesting mathematical properties have been proven over the years.

If the current boundary of evolutionary computation may seem not clear, its inception is even more vague. The field does not have a single recognizable origin. Some scholars identify its starting point in 1950, when Alan Turing pointed out the similarities between learning and natural evolutions [20]. Others pinpoint the inspiring ideas that appeared in the end of the decade [11] [16] [1], despite the fact that the lack of computational power significantly impaired their diffusion in the broader scientific community. More commonly, the birth of evolutionary computation is set in the 1960s with the appearance of three independent research lines, namely: *genetic algorithms*, *evolutionary programming*, and *evolution strategies*. Despite some minor disagreements, the pivotal importance of these researches is unquestionable.

1.2 The classical paradigms

Genetic algorithm is probably the most popular term in evolutionary computation. It is abbreviated as GA, and it is so popular that in the non-specialized literature it is sometimes used to denote any kind of evolutionary algorithm. The fortune of the paradigm is linked to the name of John Holland and his 1975 book [14], but the methodology was used and described much earlier by several researchers, including many of Holland's own students [9] [10] [2]. Genetic algorithms have been proposed as a step in *classifier systems*, a technique also proposed by Holland. They have been originally exploited more to study the evolution mechanisms itself, rather than solving actual problems. Very simple test benches, as trying to set a number of bits to a specific value, were used to analyze different strategies and schemes.

In a genetic algorithm, the individual, i.e., the evolving entity, is a sequence of bits, and this is probably the only aspect common to all the early implementations. The number of offspring is usually larger than the size of the original population. Various crossover operators have been proposed by different researchers. The parents are chosen using a probability distribution based on their fitness. How much a highly fit individual is favored determines the *selective pressure* of the algorithm. After evaluating all new individuals, the population is reduced back to its original size. Several different schemes have been proposed to determine which individuals survive and which are discarded, but interestingly most schemes are deterministic. When all parents are discarded, regardless their fitness, the approach is called *generational*. Conversely, if parents and offspring compete for survival regardless their age, the approach is *steady-state*. Any mechanism that preserves the best individuals through generations is called *elitist*.

Evolutionary programming, abbreviated as EP, was proposed by Lawrence J. Fogel in a series of works in the beginning of 1960s [7] [8]. Fogel highlighted that an intelligent behavior requires the ability to forecast changes in the environment, and therefore focused his work on the evolution of predictive capabilities. He chose finite state machines as evolving entities, and the predictive capability measured the ability of an individual to anticipate the next symbol in the input sequence provided to it. Later, the technique was successfully applied to diverse combinatorial problems.

Fogel's original algorithm considered a set of P automata. Each individual in such population was tested against the current sequence of input symbols, i.e., its environment. Different payoff functions could be used to translate the predictive capability into a single numeric value called fitness, including a penalty for the complexity of the machine. Individuals were ranked according to their fitness. Then, P new automata were added to the population. Each new automaton was created by modifying one existing automaton. The type and extent of the mutation was random and followed certain probability distributions. Finally, half of the population was retained and half discarded, thus the size of the population remained constant. These steps were iterated until a specific number of generations has passed, at which point the best finite state machine was used to predict the actual next symbol. That symbol was added to the environment and process repeated.

In his basic algorithm, each automaton generated exactly one descendant through a mutation operator, but there was no firm constraint that only one offspring had to be created from each parent. After all the offspring are added to the population, half of the individuals are discarded. Survivals were chosen at random, with a probability influenced by their fitness. Thus, how much a highly fit individual is likely to survive in the next generation represent the selective pressure is evolutionary programming.

The third approach is *evolution strategies*, ES for short, and was proposed by Ingo Rechenberg and Hans-Paul Schwefel in early 1960s [13] [17]. It has been originally developed as an optimization tool to solve a practical optimization problem. In evolution strategies, the individual is a set of parameters, usually encoded as numbers, either discrete or continuous. Mutation simply consists in the simultaneous modification of all parameters, with small alterations being more probable than larger ones. On the other hand, recombination can implement diverse strategies, like copying different parameters from different parents, or averaging them. Remarkably, the very first experiments with evolution strategies used a population of one individual, and dice tossed by hands.

Scholars developed a unique formalism to describe the characteristics of their evolution strategies. The size of the population is commonly denoted with the Greek letter *mu* (μ), and the size of the offspring with the Greek letter *lambda* (λ). When the offspring is added to the current population before choosing which individuals survive in the next generation, the algorithm is denoted as a $(\mu + \lambda)$-ES. In this case, a particularly fit solution may survive through different generations as in steady-state genetic algorithms or evolutionary programming. Conversely, when the offspring replace the current population before choosing which individuals survive in the next generation, the algorithm is denoted as a (μ, λ)-ES. This approach resembles a generational genetic algorithm or evolutionary programming, and the optimum solution may be discarded during the run. For short, the two approaches are called *plus* and *comma* selection, respectively. And in the 2000s, these two terms can be found in the descriptions of completely of different evolutionary algorithms. When comma selection is used, $\mu < \lambda$ must hold. No matter the selection scheme, the size of the offspring is much larger than the size of the population in almost all implementations of evolution strategies.

When recombination is implemented, the number of parents required by the crossover operator is denoted with the Greek letter rho (ρ) and the algorithm written as $(\mu/\rho \dagger \lambda)$-ES. Indeed, the number of parents is smaller than the number of individuals in the population, i.e., $\rho < \mu$. $(\mu \dagger 1)$-ES are sometimes called *steady-state evolution strategies*.

Evolution strategies may be nested. That is, instead of generating the offspring using conventional operators, a new evolution strategy may be started. The result of the sub-strategy is used as the offspring of the parent strategy. This scheme can be found referred as *nested evolution strategies*, or *hierarchical evolution strategies*, or *meta evolution strategies*. The inner strategy acts as a tool for local optimizations and commonly has different parameters from the outer one. An algorithm that runs for γ generations a sub-strategy is denoted with $(\mu/\rho \dagger (\mu/\rho \dagger \lambda)^\gamma)$-ES. Where γ is also called isolation time. Usually, there is only one level of recursion, although a deeper nesting is theoretically possible. Such a recursion is rarely used in evolutionary programming or genetic algorithms, although it has been successfully exploited in peculiar approaches, such as [19].

Since evolution strategies are based on mutations, the search for the optimal amplitude of the perturbations kept researchers busy throughout the years. In real-valued search spaces, the mutation is usually implemented as a random perturbation that follows a normal probability distribution centered on the zero. Small mutations are more probable than larger ones, as desired, and the variance may be used as a knob to tweak the average magnitude. The variance used to mutate parameters, and the parameters themselves may also be evolved concurrently. Furthermore, because even the same problem may call for different amplitudes in different loci, a dedicated variance can be associated to each parameter. This *variance vector* is modified using a fixed scheme, while the *object parameter vector*, i.e., the values that should be optimized, are modified using the variance vector. Both vectors are then evolved concurrently as parts of a single individual. Extending the idea, the optimal magnitudes of mutation may be correlated. To take into account this phenomenon, modern evolution strategies implement a *covariance matrix*.

All evolutionary algorithms show the capacity to adapt to different problems, thus they can sensibly be labeled as *adaptive*. An evolutionary algorithm that also adapts the mechanism of its adaptation, i.e., its internal parameters, is called *self adaptive*. Parameters that are self adapted are sometimes named *endogenous*, borrowing the term describing the hormones synthesized within an organism. Self adaptation mechanisms have been routinely exploited both in the evolution strategies and evolutionary programming paradigms, and sometimes used in genetic algorithms.

Since the 2000s, evolution strategies have been used mainly as a numerical optimization tool for continuous problems. Several implementations, written either in general-purpose programming languages or commercial mathematical toolboxes, like MatLab, are freely available. And they are sometimes exploited by practitioners overlooking their bio-inspired origin. Evolutionary programming is also mostly used for numerical optimization problems. The practical implementations of the two approaches have mostly converged, although the scientific communities remain deeply distinct.

Over the years, researchers have also broadened the scope of genetic algorithms. They have been used for solving problems whose results are highly structured, like the traveling salesman problem where the solution is a permutation of the nodes in a graph. However, the term genetic algorithm remained strongly linked to the idea of fixed-length bit strings.

If not directly applicable within a different one, the ideas developed by researchers for one paradigm are at least inspiring for the whole community. The various approaches may be too different to directly interbreed, but many key ideas are now shared. Moreover, over the year a great number of minor and hybrid algorithms, not simply classifiable, have been described.

1.3 Genetic programming

The fourth and last evolutionary algorithm sketched in this is introduction is *genetic programming*, abbreviated as GP. Whereas μGP shares with it more in its name than in its essence, the approach presented in this book owes a deep debit to its underlying ideas.

Genetic programming was popularized by John Koza, who described it after having applied for a patent in 1989. The ambitious goal of the methodology is to create computer programs in a fully automated way, exploiting neo-Darwinism as an optimization tool. The original version was developed in *Lisp*, an interpreted computer language that dates back to the end of the 1950s. The Lisp language has the ability to handle fragments of code as data, allowing a program to build up its subroutines before evaluating them. Everything in Lisp is a prefix expression, except variables and constants. Genetic programming individuals were lisp programs, thus, they were prefix expressions too. Since the Lisp language is as flexible as inefficient, in the following years, researchers moved to alternative implementations, mostly using compiled language. Indeed, the need for computational power and the endeavor for efficiency have been constant pushes in the genetic programming research since its origin. While in Lisp the difference between an expression and a program was subtle, it became sharper in later implementations. Many algorithms proposed in the literature clearly tackle the former, and are hardly applicable to the latter.

Regardless of the language used, in genetic programming individuals are almost always represented internally as trees. In the simplest form, leaves, or terminals, are numbers. Internal nodes encode operations. More complex variations may take into account variables, complex functions, and programming structures. The offspring may be generated applying either recombination or, in recent implementations, mutation. The former is the exchange of sub-trees between the two parents. The latter is the random modification of the tree. Original genetic programming used huge populations, and emphasized recombination, with no, or very little, mutations. In fact, the substitution of a sub-tree is highly disruptive operation and may introduce a significant amount of novelty. Moreover, a large population ensures that all possible symbols are already available in the gene pool. Several mutations have been proposed, like promoting a sub-tree to a new individual, or collapsing a sub-tree to a single terminal node.

The genetic-programming paradigm attracted many researchers. Results were used as test benches for new practical techniques, as well as theoretical studies. It challenged and stimulated new lines of research. The various topics tackled included: representation of individuals; behavior of selection in huge populations; techniques to avoid the growth of trees; type of initializations. Some of this research has been inspiring for the development μGP.

Chapter 2
Why yet another one evolutionary optimizer?

He who lives without folly isn't so wise as he thinks.

Francois de La Rochefoucauld

The idea of *Evolutionary computation* implies the existence of suitable tools to perform computations. Such tools have to be designed pondering the environment in which they will operate and the problems to which they will be applied, together with the chosen evolutionary technique. Every design process implies choices, some of which may not be immediately clear to the end user, but can have far-reaching consequences.

The chapter tries to motivate the creation of μGP, yet another one evolutionary optimizer. Its goal is to provide the reader with a rationale for the perceived needs and the consequent taken decisions. The text shows, in an uttermost narrative style, some of the possible alternatives faced during the early design phase.

2.1 Background

The term "evolutionary optimizer" does not indicate a well-defined program structure or user interface, exactly as "word processor" is suitable for a wide range of functional approaches and interfaces. It may be maintained that the purpose of an evolutionary tool is to automate the artificial evolution of a set of solutions to a given problem. This definition brings to light several related, although almost independent, concepts: the definition of the problem itself; the structure of possible solutions to that problem; the evaluation of the *goodness* of candidate solutions; the operations that allow to manipulate candidate solutions.

In many cases these parts are known from the outset: the problem is well defined; the structure of its possible solutions is known; the evaluation of such solutions straightforward; the most sensible transformations on these solutions simply follows from their structure. For example, one may want to solve the *traveling salesman's problem* (TSP). In this case the problem requires to minimize the total length of a path that passes through a number of fixed points and returns to the start[1]. Since it is known from the start that all must be visited once and only once, a possible solution is a permutation of the points. The goodness of a route is the inverse of its length. And it is intuitive that to transform one permutation into another one some form of reordering, such as a swap, has to be performed[2].

The straightforward approach would be to embed all this information in the tool, resulting in a problem-specific application that performs all the computation and eventually provides the user with one or more optimal results. It could be possible to choose in advance the evolutionary approach, tuning the genetic operators for performance. It could also be possible to write some information about the problem directly in the code.

However, it is often perceived as more efficient to reuse the same approach for different, although related, problems. One more mundane example of this is the generation of assembly programs for two different microprocessors. In this case the goal of the programs may be the same, say verifying the design, but their form is necessarily different. Conversely, another example is the generation of programs for a single microprocessor, but with different goals. In this case the form is kept, but the fitness function changes.

We are incline to believe that a truly versatile evolutionary tool is not available at the time we are writing. And such a tool would be useful both for the practitioners and for the researchers. μGP is meant to be able to solve quite different problems, this means that it has to be able to represent quite diverse objects and to assess them using a fitness function which is not known in advance. Thus, both the form and meaning of the individuals cannot be fixed in the code, but a flexible internal representation must be used. This is not just convenient to avoid redundant design efforts, but allows using several different evolutionary approaches for the same problem, or, conversely, to perform evolution on different kinds of individuals, possibly at the same time. The fitness function is unknown to the tool developer not only regarding its possible values, but also regarding its general form.

2.2 Where to draw the lines

From the above discussion it is clear that not all the work can be performed by the evolutionary tool itself: μGP cannot compute the fitness function for a given individual without external help. This stress out the difference between *genotype* and *phenotype*. The tool is able to manipulates solutions at the level of phenotype, while fitness can be defined only at the level of genotype. Indeed, μGP could not even map the phenotype to a sensible genotype, creating a meaningful description of that individual, without additional information. One of the first issues to take care

---

[1] In graph theory, TSP corresponds to the NP-hard problem of finding the Hamiltonian cycle with the minimal weight.

[2] Remarkably, several approaches in the evolutionary computation literature do neglect this consideration.

of, then, is a classical interface definition problem: it must be decided what part of the work is done at the phenotypic level by the evolutionary engine and what has to be done otherwise, such as by post-processing some results.

An evolutionary process is a closed loop: a population is transformed in a different one by recombining and modifying its component individuals, every new individual is assigned a fitness value and the new population undergoes a *survival* phase. After that the cycle begins anew. There is a feedback from the individuals to the evolutionary core, in the form of a fitness value. The standard practice in electronic design, when implementing a circuit with feedback, is to isolate an inner amplifying block and select the overall system function changing the feedback function. In an analogous way, the evolution of the individuals may be isolated from their fitness computation. This may be done in different ways, changing the definition of what the evolutionary core provides as output and what it accepts as feedback.

This analogy between an electronic circuit and an evolutionary tool is loose, but intuitively it makes sense. In an electronic circuit the purpose of the amplifier is to provide energy to the signals, while the feedback block tells "how wrong" the output is. In an evolutionary process the reproduction phase produces new features (the "energy" of the process), and the fitness function tells how good every solution is. The analogy should not be taken further, as the two domains are too different, but it gives a good starting point to decompose the entire approach.

Another part of the loop that could be separated from the rest is the transformation of the individuals to an external form. The tool does not know, and indeed it should not know, whether it is generating assembly programs, Hamiltonian paths in a graph or coefficients of a polynomial. It stores an internal representation of the evolved individuals, that does not contain information neither about their *semantics*, nor regarding their final appearance.

The main decomposition of the μGP approach is related to the phases of the evolutionary process involved. Every individual is first generated, either during an initial phase or from other individuals, then transformed into the object it represents, and eventually assigned a fitness value. These three phases must be kept as distinct as possible in order to achieve versatility.

2.3 Individuals

There are two main requirements for the internal format of individuals in a versatile evolutionary tool: the representation must allow mapping arbitrary concepts; the representation must allow arbitrary manipulation. The first requirement is stringent, but the latter can be slightly soften. The bottom line is that the representation must guarantee a great expressive power, while permitting a *reasonable* amount of manipulation without *excessive* computational effort. Indeed, the design of the individuals is strongly related to the design of the genetic operators manipulating them. Amongst the cornerstones of natural evolution are the idea of small variations accumulated over generations, and the concept that the offspring inherits from parents qualifying traits. The artificial evolution process must conform as much as possible: the tool must be able to mutate individuals *slightly*, and breed new specimen without loosing *too much* information.

The two main aspects in defining individuals are: what types of data are stored and how they are structured. Types of data and structure are almost orthogonal aspects. Thus, the two choices may be approached quite independently. Regarding the type of data, there are several alternatives not to limit the application scope. At the two extremes of the spectrum one may find: adopt an extremely *generic* representation that can be tight to any specific problem at a later time; embed all kind of possible representation in the tool and let the final user pick up one for his problem.

The solution adopted in μGP is to embed a limited number of *standard* data types, and let the final user exploit the ones needed. Among the standard types are: integer numbers and real numbers, both with definable ranges. A generic *enumerable* data type with a user-defined set of possible vales, like $\{0,1\}^3$, $\{true, false\}$ or $\{red, blue, green\}$.

Choosing the most generic data and the simplest possible structure, the representation would be is a fixed-length vector. Moving toward the other extreme, there is no clear end to the complexity that can be reached. Indeed, a fixed-length bit vector also allows implementing a wide range of genetic operators with negligible effort. However, while it is theoretically possible to represent any object as a bit vector, this is not unusually a good idea. When solving the TSP, one may encode the vertexes as binary numbers and simply juxtapose them to represent a path. Thus, a fixed-length bit vector would be suitable to encode all possible solutions. It is manifest, however, that such a choice would cause most bit vectors not to encode *any* solution at all, broadening the search space over useless regions.

The problem exists because the concepts that the individuals represent can have some *structure*, and loosing this information always leads to an unreasonable widening of the search space. Dependencies between one part of the individual and another are precious hints in building a viable solution. For example, if an individual expresses a function, there can be dependencies between an operator and other ones, whose result is used as an operand. While the simple vector structure is able to contain a representation of the function, it would not be easy to manipulate it without disrupting the underlying structure, especially if recombination is used.

Moreover, the fixed length of the individuals put an arbitrary limit on the complexity of the possible solutions to the problem. In the cases where this complexity cannot be predicted in advance, it forces the user to either oversize the individuals, or to make (un)educated guesses on the expected optimum solution. Both solutions are plainly unacceptable. Variable-length bit vector would solve the latter problem, introducing only a slight increment in the complexity of the operators.

A far more better possibility in this respect is a tree representation, like the standard genetic programming. It would allow to perform some recombination without disrupting the structure of the individuals, for example by exchanging entire subtrees between two genotypes. When the data inside the tree structure are of different

---

[3] Why "0" and "1" are considered two constants and not two integer numbers will become clearer in the following.

types, a blind exchange becomes almost unusable. But it is always possible to add information to leaves and nodes to prevent disruptive operations. The only true limitation with a tree structure is that it inherently disallows cyclic dependencies. For example, it would be both tricky and unnatural to represent the recursive definition of the factorial function using a tree, or a backward jump inside an assembly function.

To overcome this limitation, the structure adopted in μGP is based on graphs. More precisely, as it will be apparent in chapter 3, an individual is encoded as a set of directed multigraphs. That is, graphs where a direction is assigned to each edge, and the same pair of vertexes may be joined by more than one edge. Since graphs are not required to be *connected*[4], the use of a set of graphs instead of a single one is not imposed by necessity, it may nevertheless ease the task for the end users. In μGP individuals, some data are inside nodes. Additionally, together with the data types mentioned above, the edges themselves are used to store information. The offspring is thus bred by swapping subgraphs between parents, modifying the graphs structure and altering the data stored inside nodes.

2.4 Problem specification

Tackling a specific problem implies defining an appropriate *fitness function*. That is, how candidate solutions are appraised with respect to the pursued goal. It is not limiting to maintain that the result of an evaluation can be expressed as a positive real value, and that higher scores are better than lower ones. In μGP the fitness is actually a *vector* of real positive values, but this can be seen as a mere simplification when exploiting the tool.

The fitness function cannot be included in the evolutionary core, and there are several alternative to let the user provide it. The fitness function may be added to the evolutionary tool source code and eventually compiled and linked with it. Or it may be provided as an external library dynamically loadable. μGP adopts a quite radical approach: the fitness function is calculated by an external program that is simply *invoked* by the tool.

The nature of the problem also calls for a certain appearance of the solutions. Internally, individuals are encoded as multigraph, but they presumably need to be transformed in some way before being evaluated. Since the fitness evaluator is an external tool, it would be theoretically possible to select a canonical form for representing a multigraph and leave to the fitness evaluator the burden to transform it to a more convenient format. However, to ease the employ of the tool, μGP provides the external evaluator a file describing the individual in a suitable format. Fort example, an assembly program ready to be assembled and linked, or a sequence of cities.

Encoding an individual as a multigraph allows a great generality. However, too much versatility may be deleterious. It must be remembered that an evolutionary

---

[4] There is a path linking any two vertices in the graph.

optimizer needs to know at least *some* information about the structure of the individuals to evolve. Questions such as "how many cities does the considered TSP instance include?" or "should there be functions in the assembly program, and what is their form?" directly affect the possible operations on the individuals. The answers to questions like these define what is a *legal* individual. That information has to be provided to the tool before evolution can be started. It composes a set of *constraints* that describe the allowed structure of an individual, thus limiting the potentially infinite productions of the tool and avoiding useless computation. For instance, such constraints should not only specify that an assembly function always begin with a certain prologue and end with an epilogue that contain a limited number of parameters, but also what assembly instructions compose them, as well as the body of the function.

To maximize the applicability of the tool, the problem must be specified in a standardized format, readable both by humans and by mechanical tool. Hence, μGP adopts XML for all its input files.

2.5 Coding Techniques

The idea of maximizing the applicability also impact the adopted coding techniques. μGP was originally conceived as a tool to generate assembly test programs for test and validation. It was, nevertheless, a *versatile* tool, in the sense that it could handle the assembly language of different microprocessors.

The first fully operational version was developed in 2002 and it was composed of a few hundred lines of C code and a collection of scripts. The second version was developed in 2003 and maintained since 2006; it consisted of about 15,000 lines in C. This version added several new features and significantly broadened the applicability of the tool. It was able to load a list of parametric code fragments, called *macros*, and optimize their order inside a test program. With time, it has been coerced into solving problems it was not meant for. While useful for improving its performance, this extended usage made the basic limitations of the tool clear, and ultimately led to the need to re-implement μGP from scratch.

This decision follows a complete change of paradigm: the focus passes from the problem to the tool, and the main design goal shift from the solution of a specific class of problems to the development of a tool that can *include* as many as possible. The development of the third version started in 2006 with the intent to provide a clean implementation able to replicate the behavior of the previous version. Additional goals were: maintainability, extendability, and portability. At the end of 2010, the third version of μGP counted up to more than 50,000 lines of C++.

From the programmer perspective, the optimization tool is merely a frontend that parses options and configuration files, and eventually calls functions from a set of libraries. Thus, the *command-line* frontend provided in the distribution can be regarded as a simple example of the use of the underlying libraries.

Libraries themselves are internally organized in layers. The foundation is composed of the routines for handling graphs, taking into account all the user-defined constraints. Piled up on this layer, the user will find the functions for handling individuals, then populations. The whole structure of layers is implemented in C++ trough an extensive use of overloading and inheritance mechanisms.

All genetic operators have been packed inside a different library that make use of the functions to work on individuals. Routines for handling populations and the alternative core evolutionary process are also available. Thus, a programmer may choose at exactly which level insert his code.

Finally, two *auxiliary* libraries complete the set. A powerful mechanism for logging the current status of the process, able to handle different files and different levels of verbosity; and a parser for XML files that have been simply *included* in the project, but it has been developed externally[5].

A number of *ancillary programs* are also included in the basic distributions. These programs do not run or control the evolution process itself, but perform useful actions, easing the work for the final user. Such utilities also exploit the μGP core libraries.

---

[5] TinyXML was initially written by Lee Thomason, and it is now maintained by the original author with help from Yves Berquin, Andrew Ellerton, and the tinyXml community. The library is available under the *zlib* license on *SourceForge* from http://sourceforge.net/projects/tinyxml/.

Chapter 3
The μGP architecture

I'm afraid that if you look at a thing long enough, it loses all of its meaning.

Andy Warhol

μGP conceptual design is based on three macro blocks: the *evolutionary core*, the *external evaluator*, and the *constraints library*. The evolutionary core cultivates one or more populations of individuals. The external evaluator assigns a fitness value to individuals. The constraints library defines the appearance of individuals.

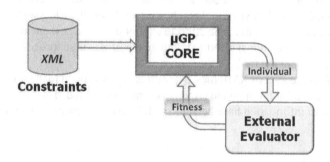

Fig. 3.1 μGP conceptual design

As introduced in chapter 2, in μGP the evolutionary core is completely independent from the application. It may be regarded as a general-purpose optimizer that can be exploited out-of-the-box. Conversely, the external evaluator defines the environment in which specimens strive for survival. Thus, it describes the target problem, evaluating how well a given solution satisfies the specific requirements. That is, borrowing the term from biology, *how much is an individual fit*. The constraints library can be regarded as the bridge between the former and the latter block. It does not define the *meaning* of the individuals, but rather their mere *appearance*. Its purpose is to enable the evolutionary core to create a specimen that can be sensibly evaluated by the external evaluator at a later time.

17

The chapter describes the conceptual design of μGP and sketches the main processes that take places during the optimization process. Evolutionary computation scholars would find themselves familiar with most of the latter topic, nevertheless some traits are quite distinctive and may be found worth reading. Implementation details are discussed in chapter 11.

3.1 Conceptual design

The evolutionary core creates new individuals by modifying and mixing existing ones by means of genetic operators. It transform the individual phenotype to its genotype, that is, it creates a text file representing the individual structure. Then, it sends it to the external evaluator and collects the results. Eventually, it uses these information, among some structural considerations, to decide whether the individual should be kept alive and how likely it is to reproduce. The purpose of the evolutionary core is to evolve one or more populations. At the end of the process, it is still necessary to extract the best solution with a tool named ugp3-extractor.

The external evaluator is a user-defined program or script. It takes as input a text file describing the individual, and produce a text file containing the result of its evaluation. All the interactions between the external evaluator and the evolutionary core are performed through text files. The choice to rely on the filesystem introduces some overhead[1], but minimize the effort to exploit μGP in a new environment. Furthermore, the computational effort to compute the fitness is supposed preponderant in the application of the tool.

Constraints are a set of XML files. They directly correspond to the user's perception of how a legal solution to the target problem is structured. Thus, *structural* and *morphological* information have been merged. Chapter 9 describes their syntax.

3.2 The evolutionary core

The evolutionary core is structured as a stack of layers, each one built on top of the previous one. Every layer provides the service for the upper ones and relies on the lower part of the architecture. The actual evolutionary algorithm, hence, is a relatively simple block that uses extensively the underlying infrastructure. In this way, it is relatively easy to change the various parts of the code and add operators or experiment different high-level schemes.

Additionally, the core regularly dumps the complete status of the evolution process, including all the endogenous parameters, the populations and the operator statistics. This is done mainly to allow resuming an evolutionary process after it

---

[1] It is though possible to reduce the overhead by evaluating a *set* of individual. See chapter 4 for details.

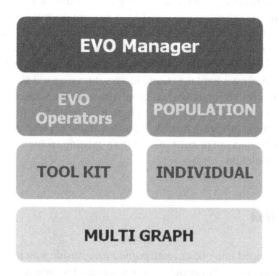

Fig. 3.2 Evolutionary core layers

has reached termination without having to repeat it. It also provides a limited crash recovery capability.

3.2.1 Evolutionary Operators

All procedures that create one or more new individuals are termed *genetic operators*. Special care has been taken to make addition of further genetic operators as easy as possible. And to allow different versions of the tool operating correctly on the very same populations, even if their cores possess different operator sets. This may be useful whenever the user adds an operator to his own copy of μGP but has to use results produced with a different version.

The current evolutionary core provides different genetic operators that can be roughly grouped into three categories: *mutation operators*, *recombination operators*, and *search operators*. Mutation operators, consistently with the terminology adopted by the evolutionary-algorithm community, are those operators that start from one single parent and create one single descendant by copying and then modifying it. Recombination operators start from two parents and generate the offspring recombining them. Search operators explore the individual neighborhood by systematically modifying only one individual parameter in a predefined range of values.

Genetic operators act at the genotypical level. That is, they cannot rely on any information about the problem currently faced. Thus, they cannot use information about the eventual phenotypical representation and validity of the individual. Thus, it is possible that the offspring generated by a genetic operator does not meet the required specification for the actual environment. Such an illegal individual is *syntactically* and not *semantically* incorrect. The difference may looks subtle, but, simply speaking, an individual of the second type may be evaluated, while an individual syntactically incorrect may not. Genetic operators may not be bound to always produce syntactically correct individual simply because the such constraints are defined after the creation of the operators. Thus, μGP include a filter able to block syntactically incorrect offspring from being added to the population. It is also worth stressing that no mechanism permits to *modify* an existing specimen once it has been inserted into a population.

3.2.2 Population

Specimens are grouped into one or more *populations*, inside which they compete for survival and mating. In μGP, a population stores a set of individuals together with all the data required to operate on them. That is, how they are organized topologically and all the statistics that are relevant for the evolutionary process. Coherently to the object-oriented paradigm, populations take an active role providing functions for higher layers in the evolutionary core, and are not mere container.

The population makes available mechanisms of selection for both the contained specimens and the genetic operators. The former selection process takes into account the fitness of the individuals, the topological structure of the population, and their phenotypes.

The fitness represent a measure of how good an individual is in the task of solving the given problem. A higher fitness correspond to a better solution. In some problems, however, a variety of conflicting goals are pursued concurrently. Thus, it is not always possible to decide if a given individual is fitter than another one. For instance, a travel itinerary quite long but very cheap, is not definitely better nor worse than an expensive direct flight. How to handle multi-objective problems will be discussed in chapter 12. Nevertheless, despite the practical difficulties in handling such cases, the idea of favoring the fitter individuals is inherent of the Darwinian theory.

The population internal topology is discussed in section 4.3.4. Roughly speaking, it may be beneficial to limit the interactions between specimen in the population, so not all individuals compete withe very other one. Finally, the phenotype of the individuals can be also taken into account by the selection mechanism. This point may sound quite weird, since it apparently negates a basic principle of the Darwinian theory. Such a complaint is probably correct, nevertheless it have been demonstrated highly beneficial to consider the phenotypical expression during selection.

Intuitively, it is based on the idea of favoring those individuals that contains uncommon structures into their genotype. Indeed, such a mechanism is an evident inconsistency with a pure Darwinian approach.

The second mechanism of selection provided by the population is for genetic operators. Genetic operators are not part of the population themselves, but their selection mechanism is. In the beginning of a run, genetic operators are *declared* and made available in specific populations. Each operator has associated a certain probability of being used, named *activation probability*. The population amongst individuals stores all the statistics of the evolution process, and such data include the history of application successes and failures for all the genetic operators. Using these statistics, the population is able to modify the activation probability associated to operators. When asked, the population is able to point out which operator should be used.

Different populations may be of different size, and may have different activation probabilities. Indeed, different populations may also use different sets of genetic operators.

There are two population types already available in the distribution of the tool: *enhanced* and *multi-objective*. The enhanced population supports several features, including clone detection and optional extermination with fitness scaling. The multi-objective one, in addition, incorporates the concepts of Pareto dominance and levelization. A third type, denoted as *simple*, also exists, but it is only intended as a superclass for the others.

3.3 The Evolutionary Cycle

The evolutionary process is performed in discrete steps called *generations*. In each generation the population is first expanded and then collapsed, mimicking the processes of breeding and struggling for survival. This chapter describes the mechanisms used to select parents, produce offspring and eventually eliminate individuals. The first task is called *selection*, and the last one *slaughtering*. The chapter focuses on the underlying ideas and design choices, whereas the implementation details are detailed in chapter 11.

In every generation a population is transformed into a new one. Both the starting and the resulting populations are *completely characterized*, meaning that all individuals have been evaluated and ranked; all the statistics of the process gathered; and all endogenous parameters updated. This synchronous, fully defined, state of the population is the defining property of a generation.

3.3.1 Genetic operator selection

The first step of the evolutionary cycle is the selection of a genetic operator. μGP randomly picks one from a pool. Each operator has a defined *activation probability* that influences how frequently it is chosen. These probabilities are endogenous parameters: μGP tunes them during the evolution process monitoring how different operators behave. The general idea is to increase the activation probability of those operators that are more useful in the current *stage* of the process. It is important to note that an optimization process goes through different stages. It is widely believed that in the beginning the best strategy is to sample distant points in the search space, while at the end, it is more profitable to tweak the solutions with small variations. The former behavior is sometimes referred as *exploration* and the latter *exploitation*. Besides, neglecting terminology, it must be acknowledged that the optimal strategy is not only problem dependent, but also varies while tackling a single problem. Indeed, this is one of the reason why sharply self-adapting the amount of change introduced in each generation brings such a dramatic enhancement in evolution strategies. Remarkably, μGP adapts *both* which operators are used *and* the amount of change brought by those operators. More details on this topic are provided in chapter 4.

There is another motivation to use endogenous activation probabilities, perhaps even more important. μGP is able to exploit a large number of different operators. Moreover, it is designed to ease the creation and insertion of new operators. Some of the genetic operators in the pool may not be compatible or even applicable in a given context, and μGP is able not to waste time keep trying them.

The first rule adopted is to reduce the activation probability of an operator if it always fails, that is, it is not able to produce *any* offspring in the given context. It must be acknowledged that the self adaptation of activation probabilities is still a controversial issue, but empirical studies demonstrate that the tool stops trying to use completely useless operators in a few generations. The goodness of the offspring may be defined comparing the fitness achieved by the newly generated individuals with the fitness of the parents. Intuitively plausible rules are used to increase the probability of an operator if it is able to generate good offspring, or even find the best solution so far; and to decrease the probability of the operators producing poor individuals.

Changes in activation probabilities are smooth. Such smoothness is controllable, but its default value usually fits all scenarios. Moreover, the user may define thresholds for the activation probabilities of different operators, bounding the minimum and maximum values both when designing a new operator and in the problem-specific parameters.

3.3.2 Parents selection

After selecting an operator, μGP prepares a list of individuals to activate it. In order to compile such list, it checks the number of parents required by the operator and picks them up in the population one by one.

Individuals in a population are ranked based on their fitness value, the greater the fitness the higher the rank. The ordering can be either *total* or *partial*, depending on the nature of the problem tackled. It is *total* when the algorithm is used to maximize a single objective function; or different objectives, but in a fixed priority; or when a plurality of goals may be expressed as a single one using an aggregating function such as a weighted sum. On the other way, the order is *partial* in the so-called *multi-objective problems*, where a plurality of mutually incompatible goals are pursued simultaneously. In this case, different solutions may not be comparable. For instance, a fast but expensive car is not definitely better nor definitely worse than a cheaper but less performing one.

The function used for selecting parents is based on *tournament selection*, that is, a certain number of individuals are randomly picked up, compared, and the highest in rank is returned. Gender is not considered, and individuals do not have distinct reproductive roles. Thus, if an operator requires N_P parents, μGP simply runs N_P tournaments. The tournaments are completely independent, and it is possible, although improbable, that the resulting list is composed by identical individuals.

The number of individuals chosen to compete in the tournament is called *size* of the tournament, and denoted with the Greek letter *tau* (τ). The size of the tournament is the parameters that most closely defines the selective pressure of the environment. When $\tau = 1$, every individual in the current population has exactly the same probability to transmit its genetic materials into future generations. When $\tau \to \infty$, only the fittest individual is able to reproduce. With $\tau = 2$, tournament selection is statistically equivalent to a classical roulette wheel on linearized fitness.

A peculiarity in μGP is that the size of the tournament is expressed as a real number. The integer part represents the number of individual that will certainly compete in the tournament, while the fractional part is the probability that an additional individual joins the struggle. For example, with $\tau = 1.75$ the size of the tournament will be 2 three times out of four, and 1 the remaining one fourth of the times. Expressing *tau* as a real number allows to change seamlessly the selective pressure, and thus to self adapt its value during the evolution.

Since the selection of the parents is a task performed at the level of population, different populations may use different selective pressure or even different selection schemes during their concurrent evolution.

3.3.3 Offspring Generation

After the selection of an operator and its list of individual, the operator is applied. In μGP genetic operators are not bounded neither on the number of parents, nor on the size of the offspring. As seen in section 3.2.1, a search operator starts from a single individual and generates hundreds of slightly mutated replica. Furthermore, a genetic operator can *fail* and produces no offspring at all. Most commonly, this happens because it cannot be applied on the chosen set of parents. For example, the operator for randomly changing a parameter inside a macro may be invoked on an individual composed of constant macros only. When a new operator is designed, it is necessary to define and handle all possible failures.

When an operator succeeds generating new individuals, μGP validates them against the current set of constraints and eventually add the acceptable ones to a temporary set. This final check is necessary because the newly generated individuals may not fully comply with the current requirements, for instance, after removing some nodes, the resulting individual may be smaller than the minimum allowed in the current context. It must be noted that constraints are chosen by the final user who is likely not to have played any part in the design of the operators.

The process is repeated for all the *lambda* genetic operators. Then, all new individuals stored in the temporary set are eventually added to the population.

3.3.4 Individual Evaluation and Slaughtering

For the population is completely characterized, μGP starts filling in all missing information. In a stationary environment, like the vast majority of applications, if a new individual is identical[2] to an existing one, its fitness may be simply copied from its older *clone*. In a non stationary environment, almost all individuals need to be evaluated because the environment may have changed and the current fitness is not representative anymore. Indeed, in both cases only one representative for each class of exactly identical individuals, or *clones*, need to be explicitly appraised.

The list containing all individuals requiring evaluation is compiled, and then the *external evaluator* is eventually invoked. Due to the internal architecture, it is not possible to foresee any order in the process and thus all the evaluations must be assumed completely independent.

In the last phase of the generation, exceeding individuals are removed from the population. This removal may be due to natural aging, or the effect of more violent competition. First, μGP select individuals that have died of old age, if any. Then, it proceeds to remove less fit individuals until the population size goes back to μ. Unlikely reproductive selection, survival selection is a deterministic process.

3.3.5 Termination and Aging

The whole process ends when one of three possible termination conditions, all set by the user, is met. The first is that the maximum number of generations has been performed. The second is that a predefined fitness value has been reached. The third is that a given number of fitness evaluations has been performed without any improvement in the best fitness. Additionally, the process may be interrupted by the user.

To enforce aging of the individuals while ensuring that the best ones are not lost the user can define the size of an elite group of individuals. The elite is composed of the top-rank individuals. These never get old, as long as they belong to the elite. Save for their prolonged youth, the elite individuals are treated exactly as every

---

[2] μGP exploits internal hash function to very efficiently detect whenever two individuals are identical.

other individual in the population. The use of the elite group allows further tuning of the evolutionary strategy.

This basic scheme can be changed in several ways to suit different needs. Individuals can be assigned a maximum age, expressed in generations, after which they die and are removed from the population, regardless of their rank. This maximum age is the same for all individuals belonging to a population. This allows striking a balance between the plus and comma strategy. To obtain a plus strategy the user lets the individuals live forever, so that they are removed only on the basis of their fitness. To get a comma strategy it is enough to assign a maximum age equal to one generation. Every number between one and the maximum number of generations leads to an intermediate behavior.

Chapter 4
Advanced features

The golden rule is that there are no golden rules.
George Bernard Shaw

Finding a good solution to a problem using evolution can be a lengthy process. Practical, real-world problems often have huge search spaces, so many candidate solutions exist. The fitness function, especially in the case of multi-objective optimization, may be deceptive, meaning that a large number of possibilities have to be explored in order to obtain with confidence a high quality solution. The evaluation process can require a high computational effort, and thus a long time to complete, exacerbating the effects of having to assess many different solutions.

Reducing the number of evaluations needed to reach a "good enough" solution is therefore critical to make an evolutionary methodology effective from a practical point of view. In the μGP several features are directed towards this goal.

In this chapter these features are described in detail. The discussion should provide the reader with an indication of what they do, what they don't, and when to use them. Some are always active, either because they are universally useful or because it would be impractical for an user to activate or tune them. Some, however, may not always be useful, or need tuning to provide the greatest benefits, so they have to be activated and possibly configured by the user.

4.1 Self adaptation for exploration or exploitation

Evolutionary processes are sometimes described as having an initial *exploration* phase, in which the search space is sampled finding the most promising regions, and a subsequent *exploitation* phase, in which the solutions cluster together within those promising regions. The amount of modification that a given solution should undergo in the two phases is different: in the exploration phase it is useful to pick samples from the largest possible part of the search space, to avoid leaving "blank", unexplored regions. When a promising region has been found and the solutions begin clustering together, on the contrary, it is better to perform small modifications on the individuals, to fine tune the obtained solutions. The same concept is employed in simulated annealing, where a *temperature* parameter decreases over time. The scheme for simulated annealing, however, is fixed. In contrast, the μGP employs a self adaptation scheme for several of its parameters. In most cases the user is able to determine the allowed range for each parameter. For some parameters, only an initial value can be set. Where a range can be set, it is possible to turn off self adaptation altogether by setting the minimum and maximum of the range to the same value.

The common criterion for deciding the necessary corrections to parameters is the rate of success obtained in the last generation. If a large enough fraction of the off-spring is better than its parents, then implicitly the hypothesis is put forward that the current state of the evolution is initial, since it is very easy to improve the solutions found so far. If, instead, very few or no offspring fares better than its parents, then the work hypothesis becomes that the evolution is reaching an optimum.

4.1.1 Self-adaptation inertia

All parameters subject to self adaptation are not modified setting them instanta-neously to any desired value in their range. To avoid large and unpredictable changes in the parameters the concept of *inertia* is used. When a paramer has to be increased it is pushed towards the upper end of its range, whereas if it has to be decreased it is pushed towards its lower bound.

Given a parameter p and inertia α, the new value for the parameter is computed as $p_n = \alpha p + (1 - \alpha)p_d$, where p_n is the new value of the parameter, p is its current value and p_d is its "desired" value, that is the value towards which it is pushed.

In general, the higher the value of α the slower the self-adaptation process, but very low values make self adaptation too susceptible to the random statistical fluc-tuations of the success rate across generations.

4.1.2 Operator strength

Mutation operators and some search operators, namely the local scan mutation and the random walk mutation, support the concept of *strength*. The strength describes how big the impact of an operator is on its input individual. The rationale behind its use is that in the initial phases of the evolution the individuals should be changed by a large amount, to effectively explore the search space. In later phases the changes should be smaller, since presumably the solutions are converging towards an opti-mum. The strength parameter, σ, is a number between 0 and 1. For mutation oper-ators, it is the probability of repeating the mutation after it has been performed. At the end of the mutation a random number is extracted, to decide whether the opera-tor should be applied again. If not, the obtained individual will be evaluated. If the mutation is repeated then another probabilistic check is performed, and so on. The first time the operator is applied without checking. The expected number of repeated operator applications is then $\frac{1}{1-\sigma}$.

The value of σ is increased when the tool detects a high success rate, and decreased when success is low.

4.1.3 Tournament size

Individuals are selected for reproduction using a tournament selection scheme. If an operator needs n parents then an equal number of tournaments is performed. For each tournament τ individuals are selected, and the best of them, the one with the highest fitness, is allowed to reproduce.

However, there is a catch: τ is a floating point number, so it has an integer part and a decimal part. The interpretation is probabilistic. If τ is equal to $\tau_i + \tau_f$, where $\tau_i = \lfloor \tau \rfloor$ and $\tau_f = \tau - \tau_i$, then τ_i individually are selected for the tournament, and an additional one is picked with probability τ_f.

In this way it is possible to tune the selective pressure in a much finer way than only using integer values for τ.

The selective pressure is increased when a high success rate is detected, and decreased otherwise. A high selective pressure favors especially the highest-ranking individuals. In the extreme situation where τ is infinite, only the best individual would ever be selected, effectively turning the evolutionar process into a sophisticated hill-climbing procedure. The opposite situation, where $\tau = 1$, gives all members of the population the same chance of reproduction, resulting in a much broader exploration of the search space. No value of τ can cause the tool to replicate a Monte-Carlo search, since the population is always limited. τ should never be less than 1.

4.2 Escaping local optimums

Many real problems are characterized by fitness functions that possess more than one local optimum, perhaps many ones. It is therefore possible that the individuals soon begin clustering around one of those optimums, without any guarantee that it is the global one.

Actually, apart from the case of toy problems or well-characterized benchmarks, this is the usual situation. When the success rate approaches zero, it can be safely assumed that a local maximum in fitness has been reached, but it should be taken for granted that another, better, optimum exists.

The following features are especially useful to allow exploration of a larger part of the search space when an optimum has been reached, although they also affect other behaviors of the tool.

4.2.1 Operator activation probability

Individuals reproduce through the application of genetic operators upon them. The operators to apply to the population are chosen probabilistically, and after the operators are chosen the tournament selection takes place.

The activation probability for every operator is not fixed, but is self-adapted on the basis of the success record for the single operators. When an operator is successful, producing offspring better than its input individuals, its probability is marked for an increase. When it is unsuccessful, giving rise to individuals with worse fitness than their parents, its probability is pushed downwards.

Probabilities are modified at the end of a generation. The success statistics for every operator are collected, and probabilities are pushed upwards or downwards based on that record. After this stage they are normalized to ensure they add up to 1. Since the amount of self adaptation is not fixed the normalization may cause some probabilities to change in the opposite direction of the push.

The user can specify a range and an initial value for the operator activation probabilities. However, to relieve the user from the burden of recomputing all probabilities every time he wants to change the settings, the initial values are automatically normalized. If the tool is unable to keep all probabilities within the specified range it issues a warning and carries on the computation.

With this self adaptation, as soon as the operators that allowed reaching a particular plateau in the fitness values are no longer effective, other operators are used, driving the evolution in different directions.

4.2.2 Tuning the elitism

When employing a comma (μ, λ) strategy, that completely replaces a populaton with the next, it can be convenient to preserve a few best individuals across generations. This can be done using two different schemes, one that copies the replaced individuals in a special repository, separate from the main population, the other that keeps everything in one population, just avoiding replacement of the best individuals. This second scheme is named *elitism*. The difference between the two is that with elitism the genes of the best individuals are always available for reproduction, whereas in the other case special mechanisms must be put in place to inject them back into the population.

In contrast the plus $(\mu + \lambda)$ strategy, originally employed in the μGP, is a totally elitist scheme. No individual is ever lost to generations passing, but only because of insufficient fitness.

A plus strategy tends to cluster solutions nearer together than a comma strategy. The first may be more useful for problems with a very narrow maximum, or where solutions have a very complex structure. The second may be more useful for problems with many local optimums, or deceptive fitness functions.

The μGP allows the user to choose an intermediate behavior between a pure plus strategy and a comma strategy. This is achieved through the use of two parameters: the maximum age of the individuals and the size of the elite. It has to be noted that these two parameters are not adapted during evolution.

When the user specifies a maximum age for the individuals they "die of old age" after that number of generations, and are consequently removed from the population.

The user can also specify a nonzero size for the elite: this is the group of the first n individuals in the population, ranked by fitness. The individuals inside the elite do not grow old. Once they are pushed off the elite by better individuals, however, they begin aging.

The effects of these two parameters compose together to provide a range of possible behaviors of the tool. Basically the user has to decide how much effort the tool should devote to search space exploration (low maximum age, small elite) or to optimization of existing solutions (high maximum age, large elite).

4.3 Preserving diversity

One vexing problem with simple evolutionary schemes is that solutions may cluster too tightly inside a very small region of the search space. Often the population becomes filled with *clones*, that is individuals exactly identical to each other. Even when individuals are all different, they may be too similar to each other.

Indeed, this behavior is strikingly different from the natural world. Here, the phenomenon called by Darwin *the principle of divergence* can be easily motivated taking into consideration the great complexity of the natural environment. Different specimens are likely to find advantageous to *specialize* their abilities and exploit a particular niche. The natural process tends to emphasize differences, leading on the long run to the formation of different species.

On the contrary, in the oversimplified artificial environment implicitly defined by the fitness function, no push toward diversity exists. Consequently, individuals tends to become almost identical, significantly impairing the whole evolution process. This has been acknowledged as a big problem in the evolutionary computation world.

When solving an optimization problem, the presence of many similar individuals provides a positive feedback effect for the exploitation of a particular optimum, thus speeding up the convergence. However, the same positive feedback may effectively get the algorithm stuck into a local optimum, forbidding the effective exploration of different regions of the search space.

To avoid premature convergence the μGP employs several techniques that enhance or preserve as much as possible the genetic diversity between the individuals.

4.3.1 Clone detection, scaling and extermination

Clones are individuals genotipically identical to a prototypical one. The only thing that distinguishes clones from each other is the moment they entered the population, reflected in their age. In the μGP the prototype individual is called *master clone*, and is just the first that has appeared during evolution. Of course the clones of a given individual also have equal fitness, since the mapping process to solutions is deterministic.

During the evolution a population may fill up with clones of one or a few individuals, usually ranking high in the population. This is not the effect of some bug with the genetic operators, but just the consequence of their reversibility. Clones, in fact, often arise as the effect of undoing some mutation on a descendant of the master clone. Otherwise, they may also appear as the offspring of a recombination operator applied upon two instances of the first individual.

In any case, their presence triggers a positive feedback mechanism: more clones in the population means more descendants of those cloones, and greater chances of recreating the original individual by the random application of a genetic operator. If the master clone is a high-rank individual, the others are also retained.

The first step to limit the presence of clones in the population is detecting them. This has also the useful, but secondary, side effect of allowing to avoid the useless evaluation of individuals whose fitness is already known. In μGP the detection is helped by the computation of a global hash value for every individual.

The user can set a scaling factor S for the fitness of every clone after the master clone. The scaling factor should lie in the range $[0\ldots1]$. The effective fitness of every individual, used for ranking, selection and survival, is then the *scaled fitness* $\overline{f_s}$. Every clone is scaled with respect to the previous one, resulting in ever smaller fitess values as more clones are added to the population. The general formula for scaled fitness is

$$\overline{f_s} = S^i \overline{f} \tag{4.1}$$

where i is the positional number of the clone, starting at 0 for the master clone. So, the scaled fitness will be $\overline{f_s} = \overline{f}$ for the master clone, $\overline{f_s} = S\overline{f}$ for the first clone, $\overline{f_s} = S^2\overline{f}$ for the second clone, and so on.

Using the scaling factor the user can decide to keep all the clones, setting $S = 1$, scale them to limit their number in the population, by setting S to a value less than 1, or make their fitness zero, setting $S = 0$ and effectively exterminating them.

4.3.2 Entropy and delta-entropy computation

Even if two individuals are not exactly equal, they may still be very similar to each other. This, too, may hamper diversity. Intuitively, an individual which is very different from all the others in its population brings a large contribution to diversity, while another individual, very similar to many others, does not make the population more varied than if it was not there.

In μGP the diversity of a population is measured computing its entropy. Every vertex of every individual, including its parameters, is transformed into a symbol. Two symbols are equal if and only if their corresponding vertices are equal, referring to the same macro, and with the same parameters. The complete population is then transformed into a message, and the entropy of that message is computed. The higher the entropy, and the greater the number of distinct symbols inside the message, the higher the diversity.

In formulas, the entropy of the population is computed as

$$H = \sum_{j=1}^{N} p_j \frac{1}{ln(p_j)} \tag{4.2}$$

In this formula H indicates the total entropy value for the population. In the sum p_j is the probability of occurrence of the j-th symbol in the entire population, and N is the number of distinct symbols in the population. It is important to note that N is not the sum of the number of vertices of all individuals in the population, because if a vertex repeats it is only considered once. The fact that a vertex repeats several times only affects its occurrence probability.

To measure the contribution of every individual to population diversity the entropy is used again. Not the entropy of the individual, though, but the contribution of that individual to the total entropy. The *delta-entropy* of an individual is the difference between the entropy of the complete population and the entropy of the population without that individual.

In formulas

$$\Delta H_i = \sum_{j=1}^{N} p_j \frac{1}{ln(p_j)} - \sum_{j=1}^{N^i} p_j^i \frac{1}{ln(p_j^i)} \tag{4.3}$$

In this equation N^i is the total number of symbols in the population after individual i is removed, and p_j^i is the resulting probability for the j-th symbol.

The μGP computes the delta-entropy of every individual when it needs to perform selection inside a population. When comparing two individuals, if their fitness is equal, the one with a higher delta-entropy is preferred.

4.3.3 Fitness holes

When comparing two individuals in a tournament selection the most universally used criterion is their fitness. The use of the fitness as the exclusive means of selection polarizes the evolution towards the highest-rank part of the population. In most cases this is the desired situation, but there are instances where it could lead to unsatisfactory results.

One such possibility is *bloating*, the unorderly growth of the individual genomes, and consequently of their external representations. Bloating occurs when individuals with a more complex structure than the others in the population are able to get some, perhaps very small, competitive advantage upon the others. It may happen that individuals grow far beyond what is considered a reasonable size to gain some marginal fitness increase.

One simple but highly effective solution to this problem is a so-called *fitness hole*. In its original formulation by Riccardo Poli, the fitness hole affects the selection probability of the individuals. With probability p, the selection criterion for tournaments is not the fitness, but the size of the individuals: the smallest individual is chosen for reproduction, not the fittest one. The name fitness hole derives from the fact that this is a hole in the probability distribution that rules selection.

In μGP the fitness hole is used to preserve diversity rather than keep individuals small. The delta entropy (ΔH) can be used to introduce in the selection scheme an *entropy fitness hole*. This means that, with a certain probability p_h, the selecting criterion of the tournament selection is not the fitness but the delta entropy of the individuals.

It should be noted that the fitness holes are never used in the survival phase, but only during selection.

4.3.4 Population topology and multiple populations

Limiting the possible interactions between the individuals has been acknowledged to be effective to reduce the proliferation of clones inside a population. The *topology* of a population defines how individual are allowed to interact. That is, to compete for mating and survival. At the two extremes are: a completely unstructured environment, where every individual is able to interact with every other one; a completely structured environment, where a given specimen can interplay only with a fixed set of *neighbors* occupying specific places. Considering breeding alone, the former situation can be seen as an example of *panmixia*, and the population is consequently, although rather infrequently, denoted as *panmictic*. The latter case is commonly called a *latex*. While latex-based population have been demonstrated able to favor the preservation of diversity during evolution, it must be noted that they are not frequently exploited in real-world applications.

A different, and perhaps the most used, method to keep individuals different from each other is to isolate them into different populations. Indeed, inside a panmictic population individuals in the long run tend to become similar because they continuously exchange genetic material, and also because they compete against all the others in the population.

Individuals can be pushed off the population even when they are relatively near to a good local optimum, or to the global one, just because other individuals are very close to another, perhaps lower, peak. The evolutionary process, however, is not finalistic: it just rewards better fitness, and does not automatically direct to the global optimum.

The use of multiple populations is a means of isolating groups of individuals from each other, allowing independent evolution inside every population. In the classical schemes, the populations exchange a limited amount of genetic material through the implementation of *migrants*. After a certain number of generations of independent evolution, some individuals are picked from every population, and are given the chance to enter other populations. In one such scheme, named *island model* because it is loosely inspired by the ancient Hawaiian society, the best individuals of each population are gathered in a temporary set and compared to each other. The overall winner enters the other populations. The time between these interactions is sometimes called an *epoch*, or an *era*.

The island model, as other multi-population schemes, can be seen as a single population structured in a special latex. However, from a mere practical perspective, in μGP it is preferable to implement them as multiple populations[1].

Different, more complex, forms of interplay have been studied and exploited.

4.4 Coping with the real problems

Real-world problems are almost invariably complex ones, and this complexity can have different faces. One part of the story may be that the solution to the target problem must comply with an existing work environment. The solutions have to be expressed with a given format and formalism, their quality must be assessed using standard tools and metrics, or the evolutionary process has to be otherwise integrated with existing software.

Another aspect of complexity can be computational. Solution evaluation for some problems is a lengthy process, requiring large computational resources. This means long evaluation times, and even longer evolutionary processes.

A third challenge may be the evaluation result itself. The quality of a given solution may not be accurately captured using just one numeric parameter. Sometimes conflicting goals should be balanced against each other, other times the main goal may be easier to reach if other, approximate measurements, are performed and used to direct the evolutionary process. Sometimes it is more effective to begin solving the approximate problem and then use the solutions obtained as a start for the real problem.

A perfect example for all three faces of complexity is the generation of test programs for microprocessors. The programs must conform not only to the assembly language syntax, but also to the operating environment used on the processor. Furthermore, the effectiveness of those programs, expressed in terms of fault coverage, has to be computed using existing, often commercial, tools. The evolutionary loop

---

[1] The basic distribution of μGP includes a panmictic population, supports the existence of multiple populations, possibly with different constraints, and implements some mechanism for copying individuals from one population to another one.

has to include part of the processor software development tools, as well as the fault simulator.

Depending on the processor analyzed, the evaluation of a test program can take as little as a few seconds or as much as several minutes.

Finally, a test program is not only characterized by its fault coverage, but also by its code and data size and by the time the real processor would take to execute it. The first goal is in contrast with the others. Another worthwhile consideration is that often it is possible to obtain an approximate evaluation of a test program performing a logic simulation at a higher level of abstraction, for example at RT-level, obtaining the coverage metrics on the HDL code describing the processor. It is also possible, although longer, to execute a logic simulation at gate-level, computing the toggle activity inside the circuit. Both activities are one or two orders of magnitude faster than a full fault simulation, so using them as a first step may be useful to avoid wasting time on expensive simulations of nearly useless individuals.

The μGP provides support for the use of external tools in its architecture. Actually, this is one of the constraints that shaped it, as already discussed in chapter 3. The use of approximate problems as the basis for a challenging one is not subject to easy automation: no amount of tool support can currently substitute user intelligence, and the two problems may look very different from each other.

The μGP provides a limited support for the parallel evaluation of different solutions, and for the use of multiple metrics in a single evaluation.

4.4.1 Parallel fitness evaluation

The most direct way to speed up the evolutionary process when the execution time is dominated by fitness evaluation is to evaluate more than one individual in parallel. This strategy is possible when more than one machine or processor is available for fitness evaluation. It must also be possible to run multiple copies of the evaluation tool. In the case of commercial simulators the number of available licences may limit the effectiveness of the approach.

The reason why this strategy works is that for every generation many evaluations have to be performed. The important performance parameter, then, becomes the throughput of the system, rather than the latency in the execution of a single task.

μGP does not directly provide any facility for parallel execution. It provides, instead, a mechanism to generate an ordered set of solutions for evaluation. The only constraint is that the fitness file must contain all the fitnesses in the same order as the individuals provided. It is the responsibility of the external evaluator to set up, if necessary, and use a parallel execution environment.

The order of the individuals generated is reflected in the command line with wich the evalator is run, and is stored in the file `individualsToEvaluate.txt` inside the run directory.

Full details on this topic can be found in chapter 7.

4.4.2 Multiple fitness

Problems in which different, conflicting goals should be obtained are common in practice. Most optimization tools, however, can only handle one parameter at a time. In evolutionary computation this means that only a single numeric fitness can be optimized.

The classical way to overcome this obstacle is to generate a composite, sometimes very complex, function of the different optimization parameters and merge them in a single numeric index. This methodology has two drawbacks, however. The first is that the problem must be well characterized, at least in terms of the relative importance of its goals, if the user is to be able to write a sensible composition function. The second is that the details of this function (for instance, the exact value of its parameters) depend on the optimizer as well as on the problem, and it takes very much experience to set them in an effective way.

In μGP there is a simple way to express different metrics relative to a single solution. It is enough to put them together in a single set of numeric indices. In practice, the computed fitness are written as floating point numbers inside a fitness file. To make comparisons between individuals possible, all individuals in a population must have the same number of fitness parameters.

Depending on the population type used, the meaning of the fitness parameters is different. In the case of an enhanced population the first fitness is the most important, and it should express the primary goal. If two individuals have their first fitness equal, then the second is compared, and so on. The list of fitness parameters could be considered a string of symbols, each symbol corresponding to a floating point number. The fitnesses are then compared lexicographically.

If the multi-objective population is used, in contrast, there is no concept of a primary fitness. All parameters are weighted equally, and the concepts of Pareto dominance and leveling are used. If all the fitness parameters for an individual A are less than or equal to those for an individual B, with at least one strict inequality, then the individual B dominates individual A. If at least one parameter for individual A is less than the corresponding parameter for individual B, and another parameter is greater, then the two individuals are neither better nor worse than the other. The ordering relationship in multi-objective populations is partial.

Depending on the problem, the use of one or the other population type may be more suitable. Details on this topic are provided in chapter 3.

Chapter 5
Performing an evolutionary run

A journey of a thousand miles must begin with a single step.

Lao-Tzu

In this chapter, we describe how an evolutionary run must be configured in order to cope with the main requirements the μGP needs.

In particular, in this chapter a complete evolutionary experiment is described highlighting the work flow required to carry out an evolutionary trial. In order to provide the user with enough information to launch his/her own experiments, in the following the main structure as well as the basic options of the principal elements involved in an evolutionary run are described.

As mentioned before, an evolutionary experiment requires that the user externally provides the μGP with a series of information that strictly depends on the particularities of the faced problem. In general terms, the users are expected to describe the general behavior the evolutionary run must follow in their experiments, the main characteristics of the population or populations evolved during each run, the interface with the external evaluator and finally, the library of constraints describing the individual syntax.

In order to facilitate the way the μGP interacts whit the outside world without harming portability, the configuration files must be described using XML with XSLT. Proceeding in this way, the user is allowed to inspect input files through the use of graphical tools, available on many platforms. In addition, intermediate files produced by the μGP in order to support its internal status during an evolutionary run, such as populations, operator statistics, etc., are also created using the XML. Nevertheless, XML cannot be used to generate normal output files, an individual for example, since individual format must comply with specific requirements defined by the external evaluator.

As graphically described in figure 5.1, μGP requires the compilation of three different files in order to correctly perform an experiment:

- μGP settings: (`ugp3.settings.xml`)
  Herein the general information about the behavior the μGP presents during the evolution is placed, e.g., μ and λ values, steady state conditions, etc. Additionally, one or more references to the population or populations to evolve during

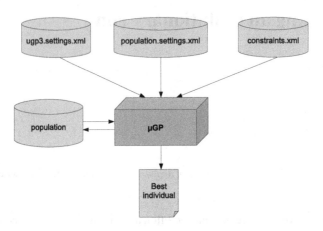

Fig. 5.1 Tool Framework

the evolutionary run is contained in this file. Finally, the verbosity level of the algorithm is also declared here.

- Population: (population.settings.xml)
  For every population that is evolved during the current experiment there is a file that contains information about the population. Every population file describes genetic parameters, as well as genetic operators and their probabilities to be applied, and also basic information regarding the external evaluator for the specific population. It is important to note that the most of the examples reported here use only one population, however, μGP has been designed to handle more than one population. In addition, the reference for the library of constraints is contained in this configuration files too.

- Library of constraints: (constraints.xml)
  As mentioned previously, the structure, content and syntax an individual must obey is described in a particular file limiting the degrees of liberty of the evolutionary tool at the moment of describe its individuals. It is important to note that due to its important and complexity, a complete description of the constraints library is left to chapter 9.

Once every single file has been correctly completed, it is enough to launch the μGP executable file by typing in the command line the following without parameters:

    ugp3

The evolutionary tool automatically searches for the three configuration files in the current directory, looking for the configuration parameters contained in every one of them. Then, the experiment runs adopting the guidelines describe in the configuration files until a stop condition is reached. Finally, using the μGP extractor tool, described later, the user can easily obtain the resulting individuals from the evolutionary run.

At this point, it is important to highlight that the user cannot only launch, but configure the μGP using the command line (please, refer to chapter 6 for more information about launching the μGP using the command line), however, as the reader will note later, every evolutionary run is configured by setting a large number of parameters and switches that make it difficult to launch the μGP defining every single element through the command line. Additionally, not all available parameters are configurable by using the command line. As a matter of fact, the μGP provides the users with a more easily configuration mechanism based on the set of related configuration files, as briefly described.

In the following sections, more detailed information is provided with respect to the μGP configuration. In order to proceed in an user friendly way, an example is used to guide the user into the μGP configuration particularities.

5.1 Robot Pathfinder

In this experiment every individual represents a pathfinder robot that aims at finding the best trajectory between two points demarcated at the internal of a squared arena. Some difficulties arise to the pathfinder robots since the arena space is delimited with some obstacles, figure 5.2 graphically shows the challenge the robot faces in this experiment.

The possible movements allowed to every individual are basically described in the following:

- Forward movement: The robot performs a forward movement following the current pathfinder trajectory. The step size is defined by a real number delimited by the user.
- Rotation: The robot rotates in one of two possible directions clockwise or counterclockwise a number of radiants determined by a real value ranging from $-\pi$ to π.

Every individual is then easily described as a piece of code listing a series of instructions encoding the couple of robot movements described above. Then, in order to evaluate every individual, the robot is placed in the start point (*Start point* - figure 5.2) and then, the list of encoded instructions is sequentially executed in order to determine the position finally reached by the robot under consideration.

In a first launch, the fitness value for every individual is determined by the *Euclidean Distance* between the final point reached by the robot and the goal point (FPED) (*Goal point* - figure 5.2). In order to comply with the μGP requirements for the fitness values, the provided values must be positive and, it must be highlighted

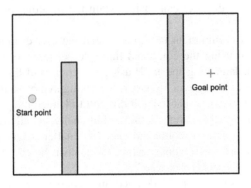

Fig. 5.2 Robot pathfinder arena

that the bigger the fitness the better. Thus, the provided fitness values to μGP are calculated in this way: $150 - \text{FPED}$.

Figure 5.3 depicts a view of the fitness landscape of the presented experiment.

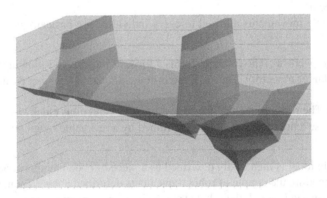

Fig. 5.3 Fitness Landscape

In order to provide the μGP with a adequate fitness, the algorithm's goal is to minimize the Euclidean distance between the final point (*Goal point* - figure 5.2) and the reached point by the robot. As depicted in the figure, the fitness landscape presents a couple of local minimum near the walls that obstruct the robot trajectory. Remarkably, the algorithm must be able to overcome these local minimum in order to reach the global minimum represented in the figure by the point labeled as goal point.

5.2 μGP Settings

As briefly described before, the μGP settings are placed in the file ugp3.settings. xml; the file is structured in three different contexts, as illustrated in the following:

- *algorithm evolution* in this context, the user defines three basic parameters:
  - *random seed*: the user can provide every evolutionary launch with a specific seed number, an integer, in order to initialize the pseudo-random functions exploited during the experiment. In this way, the experiments performed by the μGP can be easily repeated by launching a new experiment in the same conditions containing the same seed. However, in the case the user decides to do not provide the μGP with a random seed, the evolutionary core initializes the pseudo-random functions resorting to the system clock.
  - *populations*: the user defines the path and the file name containing the population options for the evolutionary run to be launched. It is interesting to note that for one evolutionary experiment, more than one population can be defined.
  - *statistics*: the experiment statistics are also saved in a file defined here.

The following code lines show the initialization of the file ugp3.settings.xml described here for the mentioned experiment. The presented lines include the initialization ones for the settings file. It is interesting tho highlight the line <settings> that initializes the option settings for the current experiment. Comments where omitted in order to minimize the presented code lines here.

```
<?xml version="1.0" encoding="utf-8" ?>
<settings>
 <context name="evolution">
  <option name="randomSeed" value="1"
           type="integer"/>
  <option name="populations">
    <population name="name_population1"
           value="population.settings.xml"/>
  </option>
  <option name="statisticsPathName"
           value="statistics.xml" type="string"/>
 </context>
```

In the second context defined in the settings file, the next options are specified:

- *algorithm recovery*: in this context, the user defines the file name used to save the status of the algorithm during the current experiment, as well as some interesting options used by the μGP for saving and recovering information.

  - *recoveryOutput*: this option states the file name used to save the experiment status after every generation.
  - *recoveryOverwriteOutput*: setting this option to `true`, the evolutionary core overwrites the previous status file, otherwise the status file is saved using a different file.
  - *recoveryDiscardFitness*: when recovering an experiment, this option avoids the evolutionary core to asks the external evaluator to recalculate the fitness values for the recovered population of individuals. On the other hand, if this option is set to `false` the evolutionary core maintains the fitness values contained in the recovery file that is uploaded at the beginning of the experiment.

In the following lines, the recovery context of the `ugp3.settings.xml` file are detailed:

```
<context name="recovery">
<option name="recoveryOutput" value="status.xml"
        type="string"/>
<option name="recoveryOverwriteOutput" value="true"
        type="boolean"/>
<option name="recoveryDiscardFitness" value="true"
        type="boolean"/>
</context>
```

The last section contained in the settings file is the `logging` context, in this part of the configuration file, the user defines the level of information the μGP must produce in output.

- *algorithm logging*: the options in this context allow the user to decide the information level presented by the μGP in output during the current experiment; the options configure the information level for the standard output as well as for a different output such as an output file.

The next xml lines complete the `ugp3.settings.xml` file for the proposed robot pathfinder experiment; firstly, the *logging* context is reported choosing two different streams for the experiment output. The first one, the standard output is named `std::cout` and in this case, the configuration options ask the μGP for a `info` level of information in a plain format. The second output is directed to a file called `debug.log` and the information level is deeper, again in a plain format. The final line `</settings>` concludes the `ugp3.settings.xml` file by closing the initially opened option `settings`.

```
<context name="logging">
<option name="std::cout" value="info; plain"/>
<option name="debug.log" value="debug; plain"/>
```

```
</context>
</settings>
```

5.3 Population Settings

Every evolutionary run can define one or more populations to be evolved during the current experiment as outlined before, and for every population there exists a specific file that defines the configuration parameters for its own evolution.

As detailed in the chapter 3, the population can assume one out of two different types: enhanced and multi-objective. It is important to note that depending on the population type, the evolution performs in different ways; clearly, influenced also by the configuration of the rest parameters belonging to this file. Thus, the population type parameter opens the `population.settings.xml` file.

Concerning the robot pathfinder problem faced in this section, the population type selected for this experiment is *enhanced*, and in the following, the most of the parameters handling the evolution of this kind of population are described:

- *Population parameters*

    - μ this evolutionary parameter is, as usual, the size of the population. However, since the population may vary its dimension during the evolution, μ actually represents the maximum size of the population. For the current example, the chosen value for μ is 10.
    - λ in the case of the μGP, λ indicates the number of genetic operators applied at every generation. For this population, this values is set to 15.
    - ν is the initial size of the population for the current experiment. At the beginning of the current experiment, ν random individuals are generated to start the evolutionary run. In the case ν is lower than μ, the evolutionary core completes the expected population adding the individuals necessary to complete μ. On the contrary, if ν is larger than μ, the best μ individuals are kept in the initial population. Herein, $\nu = 20$.

- *Fitness function parameters*

    - *Number of fitness parameters* instructs the evolutionary tool about the number of values expected from the external evaluator for every individual. In the current experiment only one value is expected for every individual.
    - *Maximum fitness value* represents in the case the users know its value, the maximum value reachable by the fitness function on every one of its parameters. Once the evolutionary core cultivates an individual that reaches this value, the current experiment is terminated. This parameter is optional and should not be defined by the user. For the robot path finder experiment, the maximum fitness value is not defined.
    - *Invalidate fitnesses after generation* setting this parameter to `true` invalidates all the individual fitness values at the end of every generation, requiring to

recalculate every single fitness at the beginning of the next generation. In this example, the invalidate fitness parameter is `false`.

- *Elitism parameters*

    - *Elite size* represents the best ranked individuals that do not suffer the effects of time passing. In the presented example, the three best ranked individuals never get old as long as they belong to this elite group.
    - *Maximum age* of the individuals belonging the current population, after that the individuals die due to aging effects. In the current experiment, the maximum age reachable by the individuals is 10.

- *Termination conditions* some parameters can be defined handling the different ending events for every evolutionary experiment. In particular, termination conditions can be exploited to ensure that the evolutionary run ends complying with very well established time conditions, for example.

    - *Maximum fitness value* see above.
    - *Maximum generations* defines the maximum number of generations the evolutionary core must perform in the current experiment.
    - *Maximum steady state generations* indicates the μGP to stop the current experiment as soon as a determined number of generations have been performed without obtaining any improvement in the best individual of the current population. In this case, it is said that the experiment reached a steady state during a certain number of generations.
    - *Maximum evaluations* this parameter determines the maximum limit on the number of evaluation requests that the μGP can ask to the external evaluator. As mentioned before, at every generation the μGP guarantees the application of a predefined number of genetic operators, which offspring can highly vary depending on the chosen operator; thus, it is interesting to give the user the opportunity to stop an evolutionary run once a well defined number of external evaluations is reached.

- *Diversity parameters* these parameters activate the previously defined techniques to avoid premature convergence in the current population.

    - *Clone scaling factor* this parameter can range from 0 to 1, and if its value is different than 0, every clone fitness is scaled with respect to the previous one as described in chapter 3. In this example, this factor equals 0, meaning that every clone generated during the current experiment is eliminated.
    - *Fitness hole activation* activating this feature for preserving diversity affects the selection mechanism during the tournament selection of individuals; thus, with a defined probability p, delta-entropy instead of the fitness, is used as the selection criterion during the individuals comparison at the end of the tournament. In order to correctly activate the fitness hole feature, it is necessary to determine the selection scheme, to adequately limit τ parameter that defines the number of participants in the tournament selection, and to choose

the activation probability, called *fitnessHole*, of the selection mechanism. In the presented experiment, the fitness hole is activated by selecting *tournamentWithFitnessHole*, τ ranges from 1 to 3 and the activation probability of the fitness holes equals 0.3.

- *Self-adaptation inertia* this parameter defines the amount of resistance to change their current values of the auto-adapted parameters during the running experiment. In this example inertia equals 0.9.
- *Operator strength* this parameter determines how big the effect of the genetic operator is on its input individual. The strength parameter, σ, ranges from 0 to 1 determining the probability of repeating the genetic operator in the same individual. In the current experiment, this parameter equals 0.9.
- *Constraints* indicates the file and the path name for the constraint library of the current experiment.

The following lines initialize the `population.settings.xml` file, for the robot pathfinder experiment. Some comments are presented to allow clarity:

```xml
<?xml version="1.0" encoding="utf-8" ?>
<!--population type-->
<parameters type="enhanced">
<!--population parameters-->
<mu value="10"/>
<lambda value="15"/>
<nu value="20"/>
<!--fitness function parameters-->
<fitnessParameters value="1"/>
<!--maximumFitness value="100"/>
<invalidateFitnessAfterGeneration value="false"/>
<!--elitism parameters-->
<eliteSize value="3"/>
<maximumAge value="10"/>
<!--termination conditions-->
<!--maximumFitness value="100"/-->
<maximumGenerations value="100"/>
<maximumSteadyStateGenerations value="20"/>
<maximumEvaluations value="1000"/>
<!--diversity parameters-->
<cloneScalingFactor value="0"/>
<selection type="tournamentWithFitnessHole" tau="2"
           tauMin="1" tauMax="3" fitnessHole="0.3" />
<inertia value="0.9"/>
<sigma value="0.9"/>
<constraints value="constraints.xml"/>
```

In the second part of the population settings file the activation probabilities for every genetic operator exploited in the current experiment are presented. In order to activate or deactivate every genetic operator, it is necessary to state its reference name, its initial weight, as well as the maximum and minimum values describing the excursion range for the operator.

The following lines of the population.settings.xml file describe the activated operators of the current experiment.

```xml
<operatorsStatistics>
<operator ref="onePointSafeCrossover">
  <weight current="1" minimum="0" maximum="1"/>
</operator>
<operator ref="onePointSafeSimpleCrossover">
  <weight current="1" minimum="0" maximum="1"/>
</operator>
<operator ref="twoPointSafeSimpleCrossover">
  <weight current="1" minimum="0" maximum="1"/>
</operator>
<operator ref="singleParameterAlterationMutation">
  <weight current="1" minimum="0" maximum="1"/>
</operator>
<operator ref="insertionMutation">
  <weight current="1" minimum="0" maximum="1"/>
</operator>
<operator ref="removalMutation">
  <weight current="1" minimum="0" maximum="1"/>
</operator>
<operator ref="replacementMutation">
  <weight current="1" minimum="0" maximum="1"/>
</operator>
<operator ref="alterationMutation">
  <weight current="1" minimum="0" maximum="1"/>
</operator>
<operator ref="subGraphInsertionMutation">
  <weight current="1" minimum="0" maximum="1"/>
</operator>
<operator ref="subGraphRemovalMutation">
  <weight current="1" minimum="0" maximum="1"/>
</operator>
<operator ref="scanMutation">
  <weight current="1" minimum="0" maximum="1"/>
</operator>
<operator ref="subGraphReplacementMutation">
  <weight current="1" minimum="0" maximum="1"/>
</operator>
<operator ref="randomWalkMutation">
  <weight current="1" minimum="0" maximum="1"/>
</operator>
```

```
<operator ref="localScanMutation">
 <weight current="1" minimum="0" maximum="1"/>
</operator>
</operatorsStatistics>
```

The third and final part of the `population.settings.xml` file states the parameters related to the external evaluator as described in the following:

- *Evaluator path name* herein the name and path name of the external evaluator are determined. In the present example, the evaluator program is called *RPFevaluator*.
- *Evaluator input name* this parameter states the format of the file name of the individuals produced by the μGP. The produced file is a text file that is provided by the μGP to the external evaluator following the indications stipulated by the user. In this case, the individuals are named *robot.input*.
- *Evaluator output name* at the end of the evaluation process, the external evaluator provides to the μGP the fitness value or values in a text file which name is defined trough this parameter.
- *Concurrent evaluations* indicates the number of parallel evaluations to be performed at every time. In the robot pathfinder example, 50 parallel evaluations are allowed.
- *Remove temporary files* if this parameter is true, the temporary files produced by the μGP are canceled at the end of every generation. Otherwise, these files remain in the current directory.

The following lines conclude the `population.settings.xml` file showing the configuration of the evaluator related parameters.

```
<evaluation>
 <evaluatorPathName value="RPFevaluator" />
 <evaluatorInputPathName value="robot.input" />
 <evaluatorOutputPathName value="fitness.output" />
 <concurrentEvaluations value="50" />
 <removeTempFiles value="true" />
</evaluation>
</parameters>
```

5.4 Library of Constraints

Individuals are generated by the μGP following the directions described by the user in the file containing the constraint library. The constraint library defines the individual structure as well as the available content for describing every individual.

The constraint library is hierarchically described in three different levels corresponding to *sections* that contain *subsections*, and every subsection is composed of *macros*. At every level at least one of the sub components must be present. Additionally and independently from the hierarchy structure, every constraint library can define a series of data types customized for the specific experiment. For more details about the constraint library, please consider the chapter 9.

In the following we describe the defined constraint library for the robot path finder experiment. For this experiment, this configuration file is called `constraints.xml`. The following lines represent the general structure of the considered constraint library:

```
<?xml version="1.0" encoding="utf-8"?>
<?xml-stylesheet type="text/xsl"
                 href="constraintsScripted.xslt"?>
<constraints id="constraints-example"
   xmlns="http://www.cad.polito.it/ugp3/schemas/constraints"
   xmlns:xsi="http://www.w3.org/2001/XMLSchema-instance"
   xsi:schemaLocation=
      "http://www.cad.polito.it/ugp3/schemas/constraints
       http://www.cad.polito.it/ugp3/schemas/constraints.xsd">
   <prologue id="prologue-example">
   <epilogue id="epilogue-example">
   <commentFormat>#<value /></commentFormat>
   <labelFormat><value />: </labelFormat>
   <identifierFormat><value /></identifierFormat>
   <uniqueTagFormat><value /></uniqueTagFormat>
   <sections>
</constraints>
```

The initial part of the file contains some directions regarding the xml file and provide the *id* of the current library of constraints, called *constraint-example*. Then, it is possible to note the initialization lines for the rest of the main components composing the file, i.e. *prologue*, *epilogue*, and *sections*. In the presented lines, a general view is reported, thus, only the headers for every element of the file are shown, the rest of the information is hidden. In the middle of the presented lines, some syntax particularities are defined, for instance, it is possible to define the format required to comment lines, or the desired format for labels, etc. In this example, the symbol # defines the commented lines, while labels must be finished with the colon (*:*) punctuation mark.

Once the constraint file is named and initialized, the general *prologue* is defined:

```
<prologue id="main-prologue">
  <expression>
  #this is the generale prologue for the
  #robot path finder experiment
  </expression>
</prologue>
```

In the presented lines, the prologue for the described experiment only defines some comments. Clearly, more relevant information can be placed here; in fact, it is usually required that individuals must be initialized with some special lines that define initial conditions to comply with the experiment.

In the same way, the general *epilogue* is defined introducing only a final commented line.

```
<epilogue id="main-epilogue">
 <expression>
 #The end
 </expression>
</epilogue>
```

Sections in the `constraints.xml` configuration file start with the same name tag. Every section is named with an identifier, and once again, it is possible to define a specially devised prologue and epilogue. in the following lines, the main section is called *section-example*, and in this case no prologue neither epilogue are defined.

```
<sections>
 <section id="section-example"
          prologueEpilogueCompulsory="true">
  <prologue id="prologue-example">
  <expression></expression>
  </prologue>
  <epilogue id="epilogue-example">
   <expression></expression>
  </epilogue>
```

At this point of the elaboration of the `constraints.xml` file, the set of *subSections* is defined. in the robot path finder experiment, only one subsection is defined. As the reader can notice, this subsection is called *main* and it is mandatory that it appears once. Again, prologue and epilogue are negligible for the correctness of the experiment.

```
<subSections>
 <subSection id="main" maxOccurs="1" minOccurs="1"
          maxReferences="0">
  <prologue id="stringPrologue"/>
  <epilogue id="stringEpilogue"/>
  <macros maxOccurs="50" minOccurs="2" averageOccurs="8"
          sigma="5">
```

At this point of the constraints file the most internal parts of the hierarchical scheme, the macros, are defined. The first line regarding macros supplies the guidelines for statistical distribution of the number of macros present in every individual. In the constraint library, it is possible to define a range including lower and upper bounds, as well as an average. The final parameter of this line, *sigma*, defines the standard deviation for the distribution of macros in every individual.

Now, it is time to formally define *macros*. In the introduction of the robot pathfinder experiment, it was stated that the robot can perform two kind of movements: *rotate* and *movement*. Thus, two macros are defined describing both available actions.

```
<macro id="MV_rotate" weight="1">
  <expression><param ref="ROTATION"/> <param ref="IMM"/>
  </expression>
  <parameters>
    <item xsi:type="constant" name="ROTATION" >
    <value>rotate</value>
    </item>
    <!--Rotation expressed in radiant -->
    <item name="IMM" xsi:type="float"
          minimum="-3.14159265358979323846"
          maximum="3.14159265358979323846" />
  </parameters>
</macro>
```

The first macro, called *MV_rotate*, contains two parameters, the first one is called *ROTATION*, and defines a constant name *rotate*, the second parameter, called *IMM*, defines the rotation value expressed as a real number in radiant that ranges from $-\pi$ to π.

The second kind of movement, described in the following lines, regards real displacement performed by the robot. It is named *MV_displacement* and contains also two parameters *MOV* and *IMM*. As in the previous example, the first one acquires a constant name *move*, whereas the second one is a real value that ranges from 0 to 40.

```
            <macro id="MV_displacement" weight="2">
              <expression><param ref="MOV"/> <param ref="IMM"/>
              </expression>
              <parameters>
                <item xsi:type="constant" name="MOV" >
                  <value>move</value>
                </item>
                <!--Move by a minimum of 0 to a maximum of 40 -->
                <item name="IMM" xsi:type="float"
                      minimum="0.0" maximum="40" />
              </parameters>
            </macro>
          </macros>
        </subSection>
      </subSections>
    </section>
  </sections>
</constraints>
```

It is interesting to note that the user can define for every macro a probabilistic weight, that determines the number of occurrences of the considered macro in every individual. In the presented case, real displacements described by the second macro (*MV_displacement*), must be present twice the rotation ones.

The final lines presented before, encode the final part of the `constraints.xml` file.

5.5 Launching the experiment

Once the configuration files are done, the user can launch the first experiment by typing in the command line:

```
ugp3
```

Before the evolution starts, the initialization banner of μGP is displayed showing some standard information. In the lines presented in the next, the tool version is presented, as well as some information about copyrights. Then, the evolutionary run starts acquiring the necessary information from the configuration files prepared before. First of all, the available genetic operators are registered, then the population or populations are created by reading information by the population file.

```
ugp3 (MicroGP++) v3.1.2 "Bluebell"
Yet another multi-purpose extensible self-adaptive evolutionary algorithm
Copyright (c) 2002-2009 Giovanni Squillero <giovanni.squillero@polito.it>
This is free software, and you are welcome to redistribute it under certain
conditions (use option "--license" for details)

[07:54:31] Registering genetic operators
[07:54:31] Setting up the evolutionary algorithm ...
[07:54:31] Adding population 0 "name_population1" (population.settings.xml)
[07:54:31] Creating 20 individuals [################################] 100%
[07:54:31] Evaluating individuals [################################] 100%
[07:54:31] Starting evolution.
[07:54:31] Population "name_population1" generation 1
[07:54:31] Generating offspring [################################] 100%
[07:54:31] Evaluating individuals [################################] 100%
[07:54:31] Generation 1 -- Changing activation % of genetic operators...
[07:54:31] WARNING:: Failure rate for operator scanMutation was 100%
[07:54:31] WARNING:: Failure rate for operator localScanMutation was 100%
[07:54:31] Generation: 1 -- Now changing the self-adapting parameters...
[07:54:32] Evaluating entropy [################################] 100%
[07:54:32] Current global entropy: 7.22058
[07:54:32] Individual age (average): 1; size (average): 14.2; Fitness
(average): 0.173591
[07:54:32] Fitness (best): "F2" {0.194231}
[07:54:32] Fitness (worst): "AL" {0.154251}
[07:54:32] Sigma: 0.9; Tau: 1.95
[07:54:32] Population "name_population1" generation 2
[07:54:32] Generating offspring [################################] 100%
[07:54:32] Evaluating individuals [#########################    ]  80%
```

Once the very first random population is created, counting in this case v (20) individuals, the evolutionary tool asks the external evaluator to evaluate every one, and then, the evolution starts following the indications contained in the configuration files. In the lines presented before, it is possible to notice some relevant information regarding the status of the evolution, for example, the step or generation number reached, the genetic operators failure rate, the individual identification and fitness value obtained by the best and the worst individuals.

The following lines describe the individual called `robotF2.input` ranked as the best individual at the end of the first generation.

```
#this is the generale prologue for the
#robot path finder experiment
rotate 2.54311086748917
rotate -1.73247932705242
move 16.7230879423961
move 2.16414657770699
#The end
```

On the other hand, the next lines show the worst individual obtained up to the same generation. As it can be noted this individual is called `robotAL.input`.

```
#this is the generale prologue for the
#robot path finder experiment
move 33.4154139988904
move 35.580956241178
move 15.4130572700451
move 23.5098101825791
move 16.7230879423961
move 13.7893260744299
move 26.4508534954332
move 20.5247237689387
rotate -0.170329881677345
#The end
```

After a while, the evolution is premature terminated since the maximum number of evaluations is reached. The best individual obtained up to this point is depicted in figure 5.4. As the reader can notice, this individual is able to reach one of the local maximum present in the search space; in fact, the considered individual stops near the second obstacle, directly behind the goal point. However, results must be improved.

In a second run, evolution parameters were tweaked, augmenting some of their initial values, such as the size of the initial population, the maximum number of evaluations as well as the number of generations available for this experiment. As a result the new best individual reached a point in the neighborhood of the goal point. Figure 5.5 shows the individual performance obtained in this run.

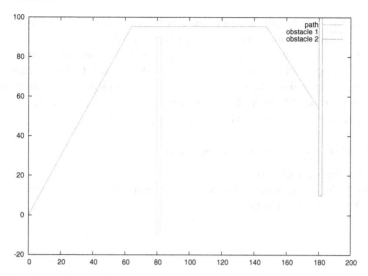

Fig. 5.4 Local optimum

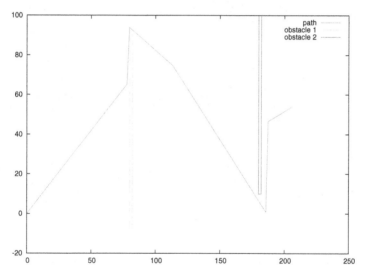

Fig. 5.5 Best individual

5.6 μGP Extractor

At the end of the evolution, the user can obtain the best individual evolved during the experiment by using an extraction tool included in the μGP distribution. The extractor tool, called ugp3-extractor, receives as input the name of the status file generated by μGP during the run of the considered experiment in order to save in an output file the best individual obtained during the whole run.

After the second run of the considered experiment, the user can use the following command to extract the best individual. The μGP extractor tool first acquires necessary information from the status file, and then, the individual is written in a file called individualXX, where XX is the ID given to the best individual.
ugp3-extractor status.xml

This action extracts two main components:

- *Best Individual* called individualXX
- *Fitness Value* The fitness obtained by the best individual. This file is named ugp3-extractor.fitness

Chapter 6
Command line syntax

When all else fails, read the instructions.

Cann's Axiom

The μGP is meant to be used either as a stand-alone application or as an embedded tool, inside scripts or even called by other applications. It has to be portable across different hardware and OS platforms. To obtain the maximum possible flexibility and portablity the tool is run using a traditional *command line*.

The behavior of μGP is controlled by a large number of parameters and switches, as seen in chapters 7, 8 and 9. Only a subset of all these switches are available on the command line.

The user is expected to provide command-line options only to perform a few high level tasks, mostly without tuning the evolution process itself.

The simplest of these is getting information about the program itself and its usage. Other command-line switches control the amount of information that the program provides the user during execution, or allow generating log files for later analysis. Furthermore, the user may choose to control some details about how fitness evaluation is performed, about how one or more previously existing populations are recovered, and finally about how evolution is started and its statistics are reported.

The user should not try to fine-tune the evolution process from the command line, but instead he should edit the population settings file, as detailed in chapter 8. That file contains tens of parameters, and it would be very easy to overlook one or more of them, noticing the mistake only when it is too late and having to repeat the run.

If any switch is provided on the command line, it overrides the corresponding setting from the configuration file.

The first task to be described is one of the most common: starting an evolutionary run.

6.1 Starting a run

The executable for μGP is named ugp3. In the following it will be assumed that the environment is set up so that the ugp3 executable is on the search path of the system.

The simplest way to run the tool is without any parameter:

```
ugp3
```

The tool will automatically search for a settings file, named ugp3.settings.xml in the current directory, and look inside that file for all parameters.

If the settings file is named differently, this must be specified in the command line using the --settingsFile switch as follows:

```
ugp3 --settingsFile settings_file_name
```

μGP will report an error if it cannot find the file or if the file syntax is not correct.

Full details on generating and modifying the settings file are contained in chapter 7.

6.2 Controlling messages to the user

The μGP constantly reports the progress of an evolutionary run to the user through informational messages on the standard output (DOS shell, Linux terminal, console or equivalent). The user can control the amount of information provided using one of several switches. These are:

- --debug
- --verbose
- --info
- --warning
- --error
- --silent

Information generated using every switch is a subset of that provided using the previous one. So, for example, using the --info switch the user will also see warnings and errors.

--debug causes the most information to be output. As the name suggests, it is used mainly to isolate possible bugs and errors in the code, and is not recommended for normal usage. Since informational messages are generated for almost every operation performed internally, this switch causes the generation of very large logs, and may have a significant an impact on performance. This switch works only if the tool has been compiled using the DEBUG option.

--verbose causes informational messages to be generated for many details of the evolutionary process. The tool will report details about the genetic operators used to generate every new individual, about fitness evaluation, about parameter self adaptation, and about saving of the dump files.

--info makes information to be generated for the same activities, but with less detail. Every new individual generated will be reported about, its fitness value will be shown, and some information about the genetic operator used to obtain it will appear. This is the default informational level.

`--warning` makes information to be generated only when unusual conditions are detected, that may point to errors in the constraints or in the parameters.

`--error` causes only unrecoverable errors to be reported. An error report usually immediately precedes program termination.

Finally, `--silent` suppresses every message from the tool. Usage of this switch is only recommended when μGP is used inside a script or is called by another program, in those cases where its output may interfere with correct operation, or when the output from μGP would anyway be invisible.

6.3 Getting help and information

The μGP can provide information about itself or about its usage. The available options are listed below:

- `--version`
- `--license`
- `--help`
- `--moreHelp`

The simplest option in this respect is `--version`, that just makes the program display its complete version information (major version, minor version, revision).

`--license`, instead, causes the display of the license information for the program. The μGP executable is currently distributed under the GNU General Public License.

The `--help` switch, used alone, makes a summary of all command-line options be displayed, without further explanation.

The `--help` option can be followed by the name of one other option, without the leading `--`. In this case specific help is displayed for that option.

Finally, `--moreHelp` will provide the user with some explanation about the evolutionary parameters, the statistics collected and the current developers of the tool.

All these options cause the program to terminate immediately after displaying information. Only one of these options can be used at a time.

6.4 Controlling logging

The μGP can be configured to log information about the evolutionary process. This information can be output directly to the console, or saved in one or more files, according to the settings file.

In addition to this, the user can specify additional log files from the command line. The syntax to do it is the following:

ugp3 --log *filename level format*

In this context *filename* is any valid name for the desired log file. *Level* can be any one of silent, error, warning, info, verbose, debug, exactly as described above, but without the leading --. Finally, *format* can be brief, extended, plain or xml.

The brief format is the default. Every message is preceded by a simple timestamp, by the indication of the message level if it is not info.

The extended format causes every message to be preceded by a full timestamp (date and time, instead of only time), by the name of the function, the file and line of the program that generates the message, and by the message level.

The plain format makes every message be output without any additional indication.

Finally, the xml format causes messages to be generated using the same information as the extended format, but included in XML tags. In this way it will be possible to browse the log file using widely available tools.

It is possible to specify more than one --log option on the same command line. Every one should be followed by the file name, level and format.

6.5 Controlling recovery

μGP can recover a previously saved algorithm state. The user can specify the file that contains the saved state with the --recoveryInput option:

--recoveryInput *filename*

μGP will then read the state of the algorithm from the specified file, and save every new state to it. This option should only be used once. If that state should be preserved, for instance because several different runs will be started from the same state changing some settings, the state can be saved to a different file, using:

--recoveryOutput *filename*

Finally, the user may decide to discard the already computed fitness values, or to keep them saving some evaluations. This is done using the --recoveryDiscardFitness switch:

--recoveryDiscardFitness {true|false}

When the option specified is `true` all fitness values are discarded and the individuals are evaluated again, when it is `false` the fitness values are kept. The default behavior is to discard the fitness values.

6.6 Controlling evolution

It is possible to control some parameters and perform a few high-level operations pertaining to evolution. When the μGP starts it reads a number of parameters from its settings file. It also reads a recovery file, if it is specified either in the settings or on the command line.

The settings file and the recovery file also contain a seed for the random number generator. This seed can be changed using:

`--randomSeed` *number*

This can be useful to repeat an evolutionary process several times starting from the same state, discovering whether it is sensitive to the actual random sequence generated.

The user can specify a file name where the statistics for the run are saved with the switch:

`--statisticsPathName` *filename*

The file for the statistics is not the same as the file where the algorithm state is saved, nor the same as any log file. The statistics file only contains some summary information for every evolutionary step, not the complete state or any informational message.

The μGP can evolve several populations concurrently, even with different constraints. The `--population` switch is used to specify the *contraints* for every population. Its syntax is:

`--population` *constraints_name*

It should be noted that this option is different from `--recoveryInput`, in that the latter specifies a complete algorithm state, whereas the former only specifies the constraints for a population. The `--population` option can be used more than once. The μGP will instantiate a new empty population for every such option.

Lastly, two or more populations can be merged together before beginning an evolutionary process. This could be useful as the final phase of an evolutionary process performed in an island configuration. The syntax for this operation is:

`--merge` *destination_population_number source_population_number*

Populations are numbered starting from zero up to one less than the total number of populations, in the same order as they have been initially created (using the --population option). To merge two populations together they have to be specified using their associated number. For instance, to merge population number 3 and number 0, leaving the resulting population in place 0, this sintax should be used:

```
--merge 0 3
```

This option may be used more than once. A single merge will occur for every use of the switch. Currently no syntax is available to specify the action "merge every population in a single one".

6.7 Controlling evaluation

The user can specify some details of fitness evaluation when starting a run. First of all, he may specify the name of the fitness evaluator:

```
--evaluatorPathName evaluator_name
```

This name will override the name (if any) specified in the population parameters file. Indeed, one of the possible reasons to restart an evolutionary process is to replace an approximate fitness evaluator with a more accurate one, once a satisfying population has been obtained using the first one. It should be noted that this name can be a relative or absolute (full) path name.

The names of the individual phenotypes can be changed using:

```
--evaluatorInputPathName individual_name
```

The individual name is the base name of the generated individuals, as expected by the evaluator. More information on this topic can be found in chapter 10.

Also the name of the corresponding fitness file can be specified on the command line:

```
--evaluatorOutputPathName fitness_name
```

This name should be the same as the name of the fitness file generated by the evaluator. It should be noted that this name is not currently passed by the ugp3 executable to the evaluator, so it is the user's responsibility to ensure that the two names are coherent. More information on this topic can be found in chapter 10.

The μGP can generate phenotypes for several individuals at a time, in order to have them evaluated concurrently. The maximum number of individuals generated at any given time can be specified using the --concurrentEvaluations option:

`--concurrentEvaluations` *n*

In this context *n* is an integer number, and is the number of individuals that the evaluator is expected to handle concurrently. More information on this topic can be found in chapter 10.

Finally, the user may decide to keep or remove the phenotypes of the generated individuals. This can be done using:

`--removeTempFiles {true|false}`

The default is to remove the files, but they may be kept for further elaboration. Using `true` the files will be removed, otherwise using `false` they will be kept. It should be noted that keeping all the generated phenotypes may cause a large disk occupation, and may even significantly slow down the system, due to the excessive number of files in a single directory.

Chapter 7
Syntax of the settings file

> *Do not assume that order and stability are always good, in a*
> *society or in a universe.*
>
> Philip K. Dick

Many of the options that the μGP recognizes on the command line are also available in the settings file. This file contains general settings for the evolutionary tool. The parameters specified in this file relate to the general architecture of the evolutionary run, such as the number and type of populations to evolve, and more administrative aspects, like the optins for evolution recovery or for logging.

In the following the syntax of the settings file is outlined.

The settings file always starts with the following line, that specifies the XML document type.

```
<?xml version="1.0" encoding="utf-8" ?>
```

The settings file contains a single XML element named `settings`.

```
<settings>
  ...
</settings>
```

Every possible setting belongs to a *context*, indicated by a `context` element.

```
<context name="context name">
  ...
</context>
```

Contexts are distinguished by their name, indicated by the `name` attribute. Different contexts contain settings related to different categories.

Every setting, with one exception, is contained in an `option` element.

```
<option name="option name" value="option value"
  type="option type"/>
```

The reader is warned that, even though in the text the `option` element is written on multiple lines for reasons of space, it should be left on one line in the settings file.

The *option name* indicates the setting being targeted. Every setting has a different name. The general rule is that each name is equal to the corresponding command line option.

The *option type* indicates the type of the option value. Currently only the types `string`, `integer` and `boolean` are supported. Additionally, every option should be set using the appropriate type. For example, a numeric option should be specified using an integer format, and with the `integer` type.

`string` indicates that the option value is expressed as an alphanumeric string. Limitations about the usable character set may exist depending on the operating system and the compiler used. The user is advised to refer to the relevant manuals. The most restrictive set of rules may apply.

`integer` indicates that the option value is expressed as an integer number. The number should be written in base ten and should be included in the numeric range spanned by the C type `long int`. For more information the user could refer to the compiler manual.

`boolean` indicates that the option value is expressed with either the `true` or the `false` constant.

7.1 Controlling evolution

Settings for controlling the evolution are contained in the `evolution` context.

```
<context name="evolution">
   ...
</context>
```

These settings affect all populations in the evolutionary run. Settings that only affect a single population are specified in the population settings file, detailed in chapter 8.

The first option sets the random seed, and is named `randomSeed`. The value of the random seed should be expressed as an integer number. If the random seed is not specified, a default value, that depends on the system time, is used.

```
<option name="randomSeed" value="seed value"
   type="integer"/>
```

The `statisticsPathName` option determines the name of the file where the vo-lution statistics will be saved. The name should be expressed as a string, following any additional rule that the file system dictates. The file is generated in XML format, so, where a file extension is used, ".xml" is advised. If no statistics file is specified, a file named "statistics.xml" is written in the current directory.

```
<option name="statisticsPathName" value="statistics file name"
    type="string"/>
```

The only one option that is expressed differently from the others is populations. It is contained in an option element that contains one or more population elements.

```
<option name="populations">
    <population name="population name"
                value="population settings file name"/>
    ...
</option>
```

The populations option does not have a value or a type. Every population element has a name, used to label the corresponding population, and a value, that indicates the settings file for that population. The population name is not used in the evolutionary core, and should only be seen as a convenient reminder.

If the populations option is not specified, the default is to define two populations, named "population1" and "population2", and associate them with the files "population.settings.xml" and "population2.settings.xml" in the current directory.

If the populations should be read and restored from a previously saved status file the option should be used and left empty. More details about status recovery are provided in section 7.3.

Finally, the merge option allows uniting two or more populations in a single one.

```
<option name="merge" value="merge sequence" type="string"/>
```

The *merge sequence* is expressed as a list of number pairs, separated by semicolons. Every pair is of the form *destination population merged population*. Its meaning is that the merged population is entirely added to the destination population, disappearing from the list of populations. Populations are numbered starting from 0.

For example, the merge sequence

0 1; 2 3

specifies that the second population should be merged into the first, and after that the fourth population should be merged into the third. It is worth noting that after the first operation the population list changes, so the second merge does not take place between the *original* third and fourth population, but between the populations that the tools finds at the third and fourth place after deleting the second.

Only populations referring to the same constraints library should be merged. A population cannot be merged with itself.

If the merge option is not specified, the default is not to merge any population.

7.2 Controlling logging

Logging is controlled by options specified in the logging context.

```
<context name="logging">
  ...
</context>
```

Every option in this context specifies a logging file, or, better, a *logging stream*.

```
<option name="logging stream" value="level; format"
  type="string"/>
```

The *logging stream* can be a valid file name for the operating system, or one of the C++ identifiers std::cout and std::cerr. In the first case the log is written to the specified file, in the latter two it is piped on the system standard output (usually the application console) or standard error.

The option value is composed by *level* and *format*, separated by a semicolon. These two parts specify respectively the information level of the logging stream and the format of every message output.

The information level can be one of error, warning, info, verbose, debug. The use of error causes only error messages to be output. warning causes also information about unusual or possibly erroneous conditions to be output. info makes additional information be output, such as the label, fitness of every individual, and the genetic operator used to generate it. verbose makes also information be output for many details of the evolutionary process. Finally, debug causes the greatest amount of information to be output, detailing most of the internal elementary operations of the tool.

The debug information level only works if the tool has been compiled using the DEBUG option.

The message format can be specified as brief, extended, plain or xml. With brief every message is prepended with a simple timestamp, omitting the date, and an indication of the message level if it is not info. With extended every message is prepended with a full timestamp, inclusive of date and time, the name of the function, file and line that generates the message, and an indication of the level. With plain every message is output without additional information. With xml all messages are putput as XML elements, containing the same information as the extended message format.

Every logging stream can be specified with different information levels and message formats, tuning the information recoverable from each one.

If no logging stream is specified the default is to output information at the `info` level with a `brief` format on the system standard output, a second stream at the `verbose` level with `brief` format on a file called "verbose.log" in the current directory, and a debug stream at the `debug` level with `brief` format on a file named "debug.log" in the current directory.

7.3 Controlling recovery

Status recovery is controlled by options specified in the `recovery` context.

```
<context name="recovery">
  ...
</context>
```

Options in this context affect the way in which the state of the evolutionary run is saved at the end of each generation, and the way it is recovered at the beginning of a new run.

The location of the file containing the evolution status can be set using the `recoveryOutput` option.

```
<option name="recoveryOutput" value="status file name"
  type="string"/>
```

The *status file name* should be a valid file name for the operating system. On systems that support them, the recommended file extension is ".xml". If this option is not specified by default the status is saved to a file named "status.xml" in the current directory.

The `recoveryOverwriteOutput` option determines whether the status file is overwritten or saved to a different file every time.

```
<option name="recoveryOverwriteOutput"
  value="{true|false}" type="boolean"/>
```

If the option value is `true` the status is saved to the file as specified with the `recoveryOutput` option. If the option value is `false` then a new file is written for every generation.

In the latter case the file name is obtained from the one specified, appending an indication of the evolutionary generation and of the time at which it is saved, as follows:

status file name".step("*generation*").time("*timestamp*")"*extension*

The *generation* value is an integer number starting from zero. The *timestamp* is of the form *YYYY-MM-DD,hh-mm-ss*, where *YYYY* is the year in 4-digit format, *MM* is the month, from 1 (corresponding to January) to 12 (corresponding to December), *DD* is the day of the month, *hh* is the hour in 24-hour format, *mm* is the minute and *ss* is the second.

The file extension, if specified, is detected and kept at the end of the name. So, for example, if "status.xml" is the name specified, a possible file is "status.step(15).time(2010-6-21,15-33-54).xml".

The `recoveryInput` option specifies that the evolution status should be restored from a previously saved file, rather than generated from scratch.

```
<option name="recoveryInput" value="status file name"
  type="string"/>
```

The *status file name* should be the name of an already existing status file. If this option is not specified no file is read, and the populations are generated from scratch as specified inside the `populations` option.

The `recoveryDiscardFitness` option determines whether the fitness values saved along with the individuals are used as they are or have to be recomputed.

```
<option name="recoveryDiscardFitness"
  value="{true|false}" type="boolean"/>
```

If `true` is specified the fitnes values are discarded and recomputed as the first step, otherwise they are kept. Fitness values should be discarded if the fitness evaluator is changed in any way. The user may want to keep fitness values when their computation is complex. The default is to discard fitness values.

Finally, `recoveryInputPopulations` specifies that one or more population files will be read and merged with the first one.

```
<option name="recoveryInputPopulations"
  value="population file name" type="string"/>
```

The *population file name* should be the name of an existing file that contains the status of a population. It is worth reminding that this is not the same as a population settings file. The default is not to merge additional populations.

Chapter 8
Syntax of the population parameters file

Stealing a Rhinoceros should not be attempted lightly.

Kehlog Albran

The parameters for every population in an evolutionary run can be set independently from the others. In this way different experiments can be performed, making changes local to a single file, without affecting global parameters. The user may even want to prepare several different files specifying the population parameters, and then switch between them by changing the settings, as described in chapter 7.

In the following the syntax for the population settings file is outlined.

The population settings file always starts with the following line, that specifies the XML document type.

```
<?xml version="1.0" encoding="utf-8" ?>
```

All parameters are contained in XML elements, and the values of these parameters are specified in one or more element attributes. Most parameters do not have a valid default value if not specified.

8.1 Strategy parameters

The whole file is then composed of a single `parameters` element, which encloses every other element. It is expressed as follows.

```
<parameters type="population type">
  . . .
</parameters>
```

Currently the only options available for *population type* are `enhanced` and `multiObjective`. There is no default. It is not currently possible to instance a simple population.

If the user wants to replicate the behavior of a simple population he can set the other parameters to "neutral" values. This aspect is brought up where necessary in the following.

8.1.1 Base parameters

The most basic parameters specify the population size and offspring.

The population size is specified by the mu parameter, as follows.

```
<mu value="number"/>
```

The *number* is written as an integer number and specifies the maximum number of individuals allowed to survive at the end of a generation. There is no valid default for this parameter.

The size of the offspring is indirectly specified by the lambda parameter.

```
<lambda value="number"/>
```

The specification is only indirect because the lambda parameter actualy sets the number of genetic operators applied to a population in a generation. Different operators generate different numbers of descendants, and any operator may fail altogether. There is only a loose correlation between the *number* specified as the value of the lambda parameter and the actual offspring size. This size will vary from one generation to the next. It is currently not possible to replicate the behavior of a regular GP.

The maximumGenerations element specifies the maximum number of generations the evolution may last.

```
<maximumGenerations value="number"/>
```

After the specified *number* of generations the evolution is stopped. The user should remember, however, that the evolutionary process may end because a steady state has been reached, or because the maximum fitness value has been obtained.

Every population is linked to a specific set of constraints that dictate the syntactic appearance of its component individuals.

```
<constraints value="file name"/>
```

The specified file should contain the constraints for the individuals. The syntax of the constraints file is detailed in chapter 9.

It is important to note that every population is allowed to contain individuals whose constraints are different from those in other populations.

8.1.1.1 Parameters for fitness evaluation

The user has to specify a number of parameters for fitness evaluation in the population settings. Since every population may be composed of structurally different individuals, for every population a set of fitness evaluation parameters must be specified.

A couple of parameters are contained in the main `parameters` element. These are high-level parameters that thoroughly influence evaluation.

The number of values that compose the fitness of each individual is contained in the `fitnessParameters` element.

```
<fitnessParameters value="number"/>
```

The *number* should be equal to the number of components of the fitness, *excluding the comment*. More information about the fitness composition is contained in chapter 10.

μGP has the option of discarding the fitness values of all individuals in the population after every generation, in order to support dynamic fitness. This is done using the `invalidateFitnessAfterGeneration` element.

```
<invalidateFitnessAfterGeneration value="{0|n}"/>
```

If the element value is 0 then fitness values are preserved, otherwise they are discarded at every generation, and the population is completely re-evaluated. The default is to keep the fitness values.

The other evaluation parameters are included in a `evaluation` element.

```
<evaluation>
   ...
</evaluation>
```

The syntax for specifying the name of the fitness evaluator is

```
<evaluatorPathName value="evaluator name"/>
```

The name specified must correspond to an executable program or script that complies with the requirements set forth in chapter 10. It should be noted that this name can be a relative or absolute (full) path name.

The name of the individual phenotypes is the input path name for the evaluator.

```
<evaluatorInputPathName value="individual name"/>
```

The *individual name* is the base name of the generated individuals, as expected by the evaluator. More information on this topic can be found in chapter 10.

The name of the corresponding fitness file is specified as the path name of the evaluator output.

```
<evaluatorOutputPathName value="fitness name"/>
```

This name should be the same as the name of the fitness file generated by the evaluator. It should be noted that this name is not currently passed by the ugp3 executable to the evaluator, so it is the user's responsibility to ensure that the two names are coherent. More information on this topic can be found in chapter 10.

An alternative syntax is available to specify the three parameters above, using the files element.

```
<files script="name" input="name" output="name"/>
```

The three names correspond to the values of the three elements described above, and should comply with the same requirements. The script attribute should correspond to the value of the evaluatorPathName element, the input attribute should be equal to the value of the evaluatorInputPathName element and the output attribute should be the same as the value of evaluatorOutputPathName element. The two syntaxes are mutually exclusive, and these three files should be specified in only one way.

The μGP can generate phenotypes for several individuals at a time, in order to have them evaluated concurrently. The maximum number of individuals generated at any given time can be specified using the concurrentEvaluations element.

```
<concurrentEvaluations value="number"/>
```

The *number* specified should be integer, and is the number of individuals that the evaluator is expected to handle concurrently. More information on this topic can be found in chapter 10.

The user may decide to keep or remove the phenotypes of the generated individuals. This can be done with the removeTempFiles element.

```
<removeTempFiles value="{true|false}"/>
```

The default is to remove the files, but they may be kept for further elaboration. Using true the files will be removed, otherwise using false they will be kept. It should be noted that keeping all the generated phenotypes may cause a large disk occupation, and may even significantly slow down the system, due to the excessive number of files in a single directory.

The μGP is able to set user-defined environment variables before calling the external evaluator. All variables, together with the desired values, are contained in the environment element.

```
<environment>
  <variable name="variable name" value="variable value">
  ...
</environment>
```

The *variable name* should be a valid identifier for the operating system μGP is running on. The *variable value* should be expressed in a format that the external evaluator is able to use. In addition, it may be subject to syntactic limitation by the system. The user is recommended to refer to the operating system documentation for further information.

8.1.2 Parameters for self adaptation

A series of parameters are self adapted during evolution. The rate of self adaptation is determined by the `inertia` element.

```
<inertia value="number"/>
```

The *number* should be real and lie in the interval [0...1]. If the inertia value lies outside of the specified interval the behavior of the tool is undefined. If the inertia is not specified a default value of 0 is used.

The initial strength of the mutation operators is determined by the `sigma` element.

```
<sigma value="probability"/>
```

The *probability* should be a real number in the interval [0...1].

8.1.2.1 Tournament selection

The tournament selection is controlled using the `selection` element. It has four or five attributes, depending on the type of tournement selection chosen.

```
<selection type="tournament type" tau="initial" tauMin="minimum"
  tauMax="maximum" fitnessHole="probability"/>
```

The *tournament type* determines the way in which tournament selection is done. The user can choose between a regular tournament selection or a tournament selection with fitness hole.

Regular tournament selection is selected with `tournament` as the selection type. Regular tournament selection is based purely on fitness values.

With `tournamentWithFitnessHole` the user can choose tournament selection with fitness hole. With a probability equal to the fitness hole the tool does not select individuals for reproduction based on their fitness, but on a criterion that depends on the population type. Currently the alternative criterion is the contribution of the individual to the total entropy. More information on the topic is contained in chapter 4.

The initial size of the tournament size is specified with the `tau` attribute. The value of this attribute should be a real number between the *minimum* and the *maximum*, including the extremes.

The minimum size of the tournament is set using the `tauMin` attribute. The *minimum* should be a real number greater than or equal to 1.

The maximum size is set with the `tauMax` attribute. The *maximum* should be a real number greater than or equal to *minimum*. There is no conceptual upper limit for the *maximum*. A very high value for `tauMax` implies a great probability of always selecting the best individual for reproduction. The user is warned that a very large *maximum* may reduce the performance of the tool.

If and only if the *tournament type* is `tournamentWithFitnessHole`, the fifth attribute should be defined. The *probability* should be a real number in the interval [0...1]. When *probability* is 0 the tournament selection is performed without any fitness hole, whereas when *probability* is 1 the selection is done entirely using the alternate criterion, regardless of the fitness.

If the `selection` element is not specified the default behavior is to use a regular tournament selection with minimum, maximum and initial size equal to 1. This is equivalent to no tournament selection at all.

8.1.2.2 Evolutionary activation probabilities

Every genetic operator can be used with a certain probability. All parameters regarding operator probabilities are contained in an `operatorsStatistics` element.

```
<operatorsStatistics>
  ...
</operatorsStatistics>
```

For each genetic operator, an `operator` element has to be specified. The probability of every operator can be adapted between a minimum and a maximum. However, exactly specifying the probabilities would be impractical and error-prone.

If the user wanted to activate a previously unused operator, or to exclude one, he would have to recompute all probabilities. The sum of all minimum probabilities should be less than 1, and the sum of all maximum probablities should be more. This would make the meaning of those minimum and maximum probabilities less than clear. Furthermore, the initial probabilities should sum up to 1, but this may not happen because of rounding.

Because of these problems, the probabilities are not expressed directly. Instead, every operator is associated with a set of weights. The tool reads the weights and normalizes them, obtaining the probabilities. In this way operators can be activated and deactivated without particular effort. This method also has the added advantage of making very clear the ratio of operator probabilities.

Operator weights are set in a `weight` element inside the `operator` element.

```
<operator ref="operator name">
  <weight current="initial" minimum="minimum"
    maximum="maximum"/>
</operator>
```

The *initial*, *minimum* and *maximum* values should be real numbers greater than or equal to 0. The *minimum* should be less than or equal to the *maximum*, and the *initial* value should be between the two.

Due to the details of the self adaptation process, if the activation probability of an operator drops to zero it will never be used again in the same run. If the user wants to avoid this he could use a very small but non zero minimum weight.

The *operator name* can be one of the following:

```
alterationMutation
singleParameterAlterationMutation
insertionMutation
removalMutation
replacementMutation
scanMutation
localScanMutation
randomWalkMutation
onePointSafeCrossover
onePointSafeSimpleCrossover
twoPointSafeSimpleCrossover
subGraphInsertionMutation
subGraphRemovalMutation
subGraphReplacementMutation
```

Other operators may be added by the user. More information is provided in chapter 11.

If an operator is not specified using the `operator` element, all its weights are set to 0 by default.

8.1.3 Other parameters

In regular operation individuals are kept in the population as long as their fitness is not too poor. To favor diversity, a maximum age may be set for the individuals. After the specified number of generations they are discarded from the population. This behavior is determined using the maximumAge element.

```
<maximumAge value="number"/>
```

The *number* corresponds to the maximum number of generations an individual is kept in the population. It should be an integer greater than 0 or the special value infinity. A value of 1 corresponds to a generational approach, in which the population is entirely replaced at every generation. A value equal to the value of the maximumGenerations element corresponds to a steady state approach. The user may want to use a greater value to be able to prolong an evolutionary run preserving the steady state behavior.

Together with a maximum age for the individuals the user can specify that a certain number of individuals starting from the best one, do not increase their age with each generation. This is done using the eliteSize element.

```
<eliteSize value="number"/>
```

The *number* should be an integer greater than or equal to 0, or the special value infinity. If an individual is pushed out of the elite, because new better individuals are generated, it begins aging. If the elite size is not specified the default is to keep no elite.

To further preserve diversity, individuals that are identical to other existing individuals, or so called clones, can get their fitness scaled by a constant value with respect to the last clone preceding them in the population. The scaling factor is specified using the cloneScalingFactor element.

```
<cloneScalingFactor value="number"/>
```

The *number* should be a real number in the range [0...1]. If the scaling factor is 0 clones are automatically discarded from the population. Using 1 corresponds to no scaling, meaning that clones can fill the population. It is worth noting that if the clone scaling is used fitness values should not be negative, or a scaled clone may appear to be better than its original copy. In particular, if the population type is enhanced, at least the first fitness value should be positive, and if the population type is multi-objective all fitness values should be positive.

The user may not want to continue evolution after a suitable solution to his problem is found. Evolution can be interrupted at that point using the maximumFitness element.

```
<maximumFitness value="number sequence"/>
```

The *number sequence* should be a sequence of real numbers separated by spaces. The number of terms in the *number sequence* should be equal to the number of fitness values as specified in the `fitnessParameters` element. For an enhanced population evolution is stopped when the fitness values of the best individual are all greater than or equal to the specified values. For a multi-objective population evolution is stopped when the fitness values of at least one individual are all greater than or equal to the specified values. The default is to disregard fitness values as a termination criterion.

Finally, the user may want to stop evolution if it is not progressing, even if the problem is not solved in a satisfactory way.

The `maximumSteadyStateGenerations` element specifies the maximum number of generations accepted during which no progress in the best fitness is found. After that period the evolution is stopped.

```
<maximumSteadyStateGenerations value="number"/>
```

The *number* should be an integer greater than 0. The default is to carry on with evolution regardless of the fitness increases.

Chapter 9
Syntax of the external constraints file

> *It is easier for a camel to pass through the eye of a needle if it is lightly greased.*
>
> Kehlog Albran

The μGP generates individuals following the indications of the constraint library. The constraints not only limit the possible structure and content of an individual, but also participate in the mapping of its genotype to a phenotype.

Constraints are external since they strictly depend on the problem approached, and therefore are one of the most variable parts of the entire approach.

9.1 Purposes of the constraints

As seen in chapter 3, using the tagged graph representation an individual could assume any possible structure that can be described by a collection of multigraphs. Additionally, every vertex and every edge of each multigraph can contain an arbitrary sequence of symbols.

All this potential variety is necessary to preserve the generality of the tool. Any arbitrary limitation in the base representation could make it impossible to apply the approach to some class of problems. For instance, hypothesizing that the tool is used to generate code of some kind, imposing that the base structure is that of a proper graph instead of a multigraph would disallow making two syntactically different references to a single location from the same instruction.

Conversely, without additional information the tool would have no way to generate the phenotype of the individuals. It could only produce an arbitrarily chosen encoding of the internal representation, that would not in general resemble the desired form of a candidate solution.

The constraints cover these three roles at the same time. They describe the possible *structure* of an individual, provide the allowed *content* for the elements of the graph, and dictate the *syntax* of a candidate solution.

All together, the constraints define what is a *valid* individual. Any individual that is not valid, or *invalid*, will be discarded immediately, without evaluating it or allowing it to reproduce.

The constraints library is provided to the tool in an XML file. This encoding allows a minimal form of validation using standard tools. It also allows browsing the constraints with widely available instruments, to perform a visual inspection.

The constraints always begin with the following lines, that specify the XML document type.

```
<?xml version="1.0" encoding="utf-8"?>
<?xml-stylesheet type="text/xsl"
  href="http://www.cad.polito.it/ugp3/transforms/
              constraintsScripted.xslt"?>
```

The reader should note that, although here they are written on successive lines for space reasons, elements between angle brackets ("<" and ">"), and especially elements between double quotes ("") may have to be written on one line. These lines, through the specification of a XSLT file, also instruct a browser about how to render the various elements of the library.

9.2 Organization of constraints and hierarchy

The constraints are divided in *sections*, each of which is composed of *subsections*, in turn made up of *macros*. Every level in the hierarchy is in relation with a corresponding level of the representation, and works as a template for the elements at that level.

Even if the individuals are represented through graphs, the constraints do not actually form a general graph, but a tree. The root of this tree is the constraints library itself. The first level is composed by the sections, the second level by subsections and the third level contains the macros.

The constraints are specified by an XML element named constraints.

```
<constraints
  xmlns="http://www.cad.polito.it/ugp3/schemas/
              constraints"
  id="constraints name"
  xmlns:xsi="http://www.w3.org/2001/
                  XMLSchema-instance"
  xsi:schemaLocation="http://www.cad.polito.it/ugp3/
                          schemas/constraints
                      http://www.cad.polito.it/ugp3/
                          schemas/constraints.xsd">
```

...

```
</constraints>
```

The name of the constraints, specified by the id attribute, should be unique within an evolutionary run. Since it is possible to use different populations and every population could have its own constraints, the use of a name helps distinguishing the different constraints.

Apart from the two header lines specified above, all other elements of the constraints library are specified as children of the constraints element.

The sections are contained in a specific sections element. There cannot be more than one sections element, but there can be as many sections as needed inside it.

```
<sections>
  <section section attributes >
    ...
  </section>
  <section section attributes >
    ...
  </section>
  ...
<sections>
```

A section always comprises a prologue and an epilogue, together with a subsections element, that contains the subsections.

```
<section section attributes >
  <prologue prologue attributes >
    <expression>
      ...
    </expression>
  </prologue>
  <epilogue epilogue attributes >
    <expression>
      ...
    </expression>
  </epilogue>
  <subSections>

    ...

  </subSections>
</section>
```

The organization of the subsections element is equal to that of the sections element. Again, every subsection has to be contained inside a single subsections element.

```
<subSections>
  <subSection subsection attributes >
    ...
  </subSection>
  <subSection subsection attributes >
    ...
  </subSection>
  ...
<subSections>
```

A subsection always belongs to a specific section, and cannot be shared between different sections. If identical syntactic constraints have to be specified for a subsection in different sections, it must be replicated. In the authors' experience, however, this should be seen as a warning that the constraints could be expressed better in a different way.

The organization of every subsection follows that of a section. Every subsection comprises a prologue, an epilogue and a macros element, containing all macros that can be used within the corresponding subgraphs.

```
<subSection subsection attributes >
  <prologue prologue attributes >
    <expression>
      ...
    </expression>
  </prologue>
  <epilogue epilogue attributes >
    <expression>
      ...
    </expression>
  </epilogue>
  <macros macros attributes >


    ...


  </macros>
</subSection>
```

The macros element is organized as the subSections element. The macros element, diferently from the sections and subsections elements, has some attributes to help define the structure of the individual.

```
<macros macros attributes >
  <macro macro attributes >
```

```
   ...
</macro>
<macro macro attributes >
   ...
</macro>
...
<macros>
```

Macros belong to subsections, and again they cannot be shared. In this case, however, there is greater scope for replication. Indeed, identical syntactic elements may be needed in subgraphs with markedly different roles. This, too, should nonetheless be viewed as a second-choice solution.

Macros can in turn contain parameters. Differently from sections and subsections, macros are treated as atomic entities. This means that there is no choice whether to instance or not a macro parameter. Once a macro is used to constrain a vertex of the graph, all its parameters are assigned a value and attached as tags to that vertex. This also explains why the parameters are not considered part of the constraint hierarchy, but just elements of each macro.

```
<macro macro attributes >
   <expression>
      ...
   </expression>
   <parameters>
      ...
   </parameters>
</macro>
```

Aside from the structural hierarchy of the constraints, other elements belong to the constraints. Independently from any section, the user can define some data types for subsequent reference. These data types can be referred to in the declarations of the macro parameters. The data types are defined inside a typeDefinitions element, with the following syntax.

```
<typeDefinitions>
   <item item attributes >
      ...
   </item>
   ...
</typeDefinitions>
```

For each level of the hierarchy, four formats can also be defined. These are the *comment* format, the *identifier* format, the *unique tag* format and the *label* format. These must be defined for the constraints element, and may be redefined inside every section, subsection and macro. No global default is supplied for their content, but once defined it is inherited through all the hierarchy.

The comment format describes the syntactic constraints for comments in the individual. The evolutionary core can generate comment lines in the phenotype of an individual. To ensure that these comments are syntactically correct the comment is output according to the specified comment format. The corresponding element is as follows.

<commentFormat> *comment expression* </commentFormat>

The comment expression is limited to the form

comment prefix <value/> *comment suffix*

where the comment prefix and suffix are specified by the actual language in which the individual is written. For example, for assembly the comment prefix is often a hash character ('#'), and the suffix is a literal newline at the end of the comment expression, before the closing tag. The user should beware that spaces and tabs are significant in this expression.

This simple expression is used also for the other three format elements. It is not currently possible to use arbitrary expressions for the format elements.

The other three elements are linked together, and describe the syntactical constraints for the references within an individual. The first element is the identifier format. This describes a correct format for an identifier that can be referred to. It will also be the form of the identifier used in the reference. The XML element is as follows.

<identifierFormat> *identifier expression* </identifierFormat>

The actual identifiers generated by the evolutionary core comprise all letters and numbers allowed in the *BASE32* encoding. These are all uppercase letters and six numbers in ISO 646 encoding, for a total of 32 symbols. All symbols can appear in every position in an internal identifier, without syntactic restrictions. Most languages, however, dictate that valid identifiers can only begin with a subset of the encoded characters, typically excluding numbers. In these cases it is enough to use an expression formed by a prefix letter followed by the <value/> tag, without suffixes.

The second element is the label format. This element specifies the accepted format of an identifier when it is used as a label, not as a reference. In other words, it is the form of the identifier when it indicates the target of a reference, rather than point in which the reference is made. The element is

<labelFormat> *label expression* </labelFormat>

It should be noted that in this case the `<value>` tag does not indicate, as in the identifier expression, an internal name of the evolutionary core, but the result of its transformation in a syntactically valid identifier. This means that the constant parts of the identifier expression should not be repeated here. The purpose of the label expression is that of specifying the *additional* constraints of a label with respect to a normal identifier. Using again assembly as an example, the usual form of a label is an identifier immediately followed by a colon. The label expression will then be the `<value/>` tag immediately followed by the colon, with no prefix.

Lastly, the unique tag format should be defined. A unique tag is an identifier that is guaranteed not to conflict with any other identifier present in an individual. The element is as follows.

```
<uniqueTagFormat> unique tag expression </uniqueTagFormat>
```

A unique tag may be repeated as many times as needed within a macro, but it cannot be referred to by any other macro. A possible use of unique tags is described in the following.

9.3 Specifying the structure of the individual

The structure of an individual is specified by the structure of the sections and subsections in the constraints.

The sections correspond to the graphs of the individuals. In the constraints, every section describes a graph that will be present in the individual. In the majority of cases a single graph, and thus a single section, is enough to describe the syntax of an individual.

Every section element is completed by two attributes. The first is the section name, identified by the `id` attribute name. The section name has to be a valid identifier for XML, and it should be unique within a constraints library. The second is identified by `prologueEpilogueCompulsory`, and specifies whether the prologue and epilogue of a section should always be present in the phenotype of the individual, even if the section is otherwise empty. The allowed values for this attribute are "true" and "false". No default is provided, and the attribute should always be present.

The syntax for the `section` element is then

```
<section id="section name"
prologueEpilogueCompulsory="{true|false}
```

Every `section` element, besides a `prologue` and an `epilogue` elements, should contain a `subSections` element, comprising all subsections for that section.

Differently from sections, subsections are not directly mapped to subgraphs in an individual. Instead, every subsection acts as a *template* for a potentially unlimited number of subgraphs.

The `subSections` element has no additional attribute, amounting to a simple container element. Its syntax is therefore just

```
<subSections>
```

Every `subsection` element, instead, has five attributes. The first is the subsection name, as usual identified by the `id` attribute.

The following two are the `minOccurs` and `maxOccurs` attributes, that tell how many subgraphs corresponding to that subsection are allowed to exist in a valid individual.

The possible values for both attributes are all integers, positive or equal to zero. The value of `maxOccurs` must be greater or equal to the value of `minOccurs`. No defaults are provided for these attributes, and they are not optional. For the `maxOccurs` attribute only, the special value "infinity" is allowed. This indicates that no upper bound exists to the number of subgraphs for the considered subsection. This special value is not allowed for `minOccurs`, since it would dictate that all individuals must contain an infinite number of subgraphs for this section.

It is possible to specify a maximum number of instances for the subsection equal to zero. This can be handy if the user wants to experiment allowing or disallowing a given subsection, without making large modifications to the constraints.

The third attribute is `maxReferences`, that determines the maximum allowed number of references to the prologue of every subgraph starting from outside the subgraph itself. This attribute determines whether every subgraph corresponding to the subsection can be referred to, and, if it can, whether it could be shared among different references. The possible values for this attribute are integers greater than or equal to zero. The "infinity" value is not allowed. This attribute also is compulsory.

The fourth attribute is `expand`. This attribute indicates explicitly whether sharing of the subgraphs should be forbidden or not. If the attribute value is "true", then the graph should be expanded, meaning that no subgraph should be referred to more than once. Currently this attribute just activates a check that the maximum number of references is no more than one. The `expand` attribute is optional, and if not specified assumes a default value of "false".

The syntax for the subsection element is as follows.

```
<subsection id="subsection name"
 minOccurs="minimum subgraph number"
 maxOccurs="maximum subgraph number"
 maxReferences="maximum inbound edges"
 expand="{true|false}">
```

Every subsection contains its own prologue and epilogue elements, and a macros element. The macros element is qualified by four attributes. They are the `minOccurs`, maxOccurs, the averageOccurs and the sigma attributes. These all describe the statistical distribution of vertices in every subgraph. All four attributes are compulsory.

Every subgraph in an individual is mapped to a subsection. It is composed of a prologue, a number of vertices and an epilogue. The minOccurs and maxOccurs attributes of the macros element specify the minimum and maximum number of vertices, apart from the prologue and epilogue, that can exist in every subgraph mapped to the curent subsection. As in the case of the subsection element, the maxOccurs attribute must be greater than or equal to minOccurs. For both attributes any integer value, greater than or equal to zero, is allowed. For the maxOccurs attribute only, it is possible to specify the special "infinity" value, meaning that there is no upper limit to the number of vertices in a subgraph.

The averageOccurs attribute is used when a random individual is built, to specify the average number of vertices that compose a subgraph corresponding to the subsection. The number of vertices is determined randomly following a Gaussian probability distribution. The sigma attribute, therefore, specifies the standard deviation of that distribution. The probability distribution is truncated so that no more than minOccurs and no more than maxOccurs vertices are generated for a given subgraph. The value for the averageOccurs attribute can be any integer number greater than or equal to zero. The sigma attribute, instead, can take on any non negative real value.

The macros element does not need an id attribute, since it is the only one inside a subsection element.

The syntax for the macros element is then

```
<macros minOccurs="minimum vertex number"
 maxOccurs="maximum vertex number"
 averageOccurs="average initial vertex number"
 sigma="initial standard deviation">
```

Inside the macros element there is the specification of every macro in the subsection. They are described by the macro elements.

Every macro element has two attributes. The first is the usual id attribute, containing the name of the macro. This name should be unique within the subsection.

The second attribute is the weight attribute. This attribute is used during the generation of a random individual, to modify the probability that a macro is chosen as the template for a vertex. This probability is equal to the value of the weight attribute, divided by the sum of all weights of the subsection. The default value for this attribute is 1.0. The possible value for the weight attribute is any floating point number greater than or equal to zero. The "infinity" special value is not available. The weight attribute is optional, and its default value is 1.0.

The syntax for the macro element is as follows.

```
<macro id="macro name"
 weight="probabilistic weight">
```

9.4 Specifying the contents of the individual

The allowed content for an individual is specified inside the macros, the prologues and the epilogues. These elements are distinct because they fulfill different roles, but their syntax is almost identical.

A macro may optionally contain a comment format, an identifier format, a label format and a unique tag format. Besides those, it contains an `expression` element and a `parameters` element. Inside this several parameter definitions, each denoted by an `item` element, can be contained. The syntax is as follows.

```
<macro macro attributes >
  <expression> ... </expression>
  <parameters>
    <item parameter definition attributes >
    ...
  </parameters>
</macro>
```

The expression determines the appearance of each graph vertex in the phenotype of the individual. It is composed of a string within which some elements are replaced by variable parameters. The presence of a parameter inside the expression string is marked by the `param` element. Every other character in the string is copied verbatim in the phenotype of the individual, except for some special characters. If the special characters '&', '<', '>', ''', '""' are required in the expression, they have to be replaced with the XML sequences "&", "<", ">", "'", """ respectively. The expression of a macro can be omitted. If it is not present, it is equivalent to an empty expression. A macro with an empty expression can be useful in order to use the corresponding vertices as mere placeholders. Such vertices, in fact, can be referred to, but do not take up space except for the labels.

Parameters in an expression are somewhat like variables in a program. They are *defined* inside the `parameters` element, and *instanced* in the expression using the `param` elements. Exactly as with variables, they should be defined only once, but can be used many times in the expression. All the instances belonging to the same vertex will have the same value, so that the user can enforce the correspondence between different parts of the expression. Every instance of a parameter should refer to a definition in the `parameters` element. A parameter may be defined and not referred to in the expression. This is not an error, but for performance reasons it is not recommended. If no parameters are used in the expression of the macro, the `parameters` element is not needed.

Every parameter inside the expression is identified by its `ref` attribute. This tells which parameter the current instance refers to. Its value should be equal to the name attribute of one of the macro parameters.

The syntax of the `param` element is

```
<param ref="parameter name">
```

An expression, then, can be composed of any sequence of constant strings and parameters, in any order.

The definition of a parameter is contained in an `item` element within the `parameters` element. Every parameter has a name, that constitutes the value of the `name` attribute. This name should be unique within the macro.

Parameters can be of several types, and the attributes of the element depend on the specific type. The type of the parameter is specified by the `type` attribute.

Two general kinds of parameter types are available. The first kind is that of *data parameters*, that is parameters that can assume values that are totally unrelated to the structure of the individual. The second is that of *structural parameters*, that describe relationships between different elements of an individual.

Data parameters are several. The first possible type is `integer`. It actually specifies a range of possible integer values. The relative attributes are `minimum`, that specifies the minimum allowed value, `maximum`, setting the maximum possible value. No defaults are provided for these attributes, and they are compulsory. The syntax in this case is as follows.

```
<item name="parameter name"
 type="integer"
 minimum="range start"
 maximum="range end"/>
```

Then there is the `bitArray` type. It specifies a value that is composed by a fixed number of binary digits. Three attributes describe the parameter.

The first attribute is `length`, that tells how many bits compose the value. There is no arbitrary restriction to the length of the array.

The second is the `pattern` attribute, that specifies which bits must be 0, which must be 1 and which ones will be generated by the evolutionary core. The pattern is syntactically a string composed of '0', '1' and '-' characters, one per element of the array. '0' and '1' characters indicate bits that must remain untouched at the prescribed value, whereas '-' characters indicate bits that can be modified during evolution. For example, the "-01-" pattern indicates a four-bit array in which the first and last bits can vary, the second will always be 0 and the third will always be 1. The length of the pattern has to be coherent with the value of the `length` parameter. If the pattern is not specified, it is assumed composed of all '-' characters.

At least one of the `length` and `pattern` attributes should be specified, but it is not necessary to provide both. If the `length` attribute is missing, its value is taken equal to the length of the pattern string.

It is possible that the bit array is subject to further syntactic limitations, such as being expressed in a particular base. This is obtained through the use of the `base` attribute, that tells the numeric base in which the array must be written. The allowed values for this attribute are "bin" for binary representation, "oct" for octal and "hex" for hexadecimal. The decimal representation is not allowed, as it would not imply a fixed number of digits. Every octal digit corresponds to three binary digits, and an hexadecimal digit spans four bits. The length of the array, and of the pattern, should then be a multiple of the length of a base digit, three for octal base and four for hexadecimal. If not all bits are required the pattern should begin with a suitable number of '0' characters, to reach the correct length. The base attribute should be provided, and no default value exists for it. The pattern must always be specified in terms of bits, not of octal or hexadecimal digits.

The syntax for the bit array type is

```
<item name="parameter name"
 type="bitArray"
 length="array bit length"
 pattern="bit pattern sequence"
 base="bin|oct|hex"/>
```

Another type is float. It is conceptually, and syntactically, similar to the integer type. It is completed by the minimum and maximum attributes, that indicate the minimum and maximum value of the allowed range. All these values are floating point numbers. Both attributes are compulsory, with no default. The syntax is as follows.

```
<item name="parameter name"
 type="float"
 minimum="range start"
 maximum="range end"/>
```

The constant type specifies that the value of the parameter has to be chosen among a list of symbolic constants. It requires no further attributes, but lists the allowed values as further value elements inside the item element. The value of a symbolic constant is any string, subject to the same syntactic limitation as the constant parts of the macro expression. There is no predefined limit to the number of symbolic strings, but at least one should be provided.

The syntax for the constant type is

```
<item name="parameter name"
 type="constant">
 <value>string</value>
 ...
</item>
```

The environment type allows using environment variables inside the generated individuals. This type has one further attribute, variable, that specifies the name of the referred environment variable. The variable attribute is compulsory, without any default value. A parameter of environment type is always substituted verbatim by the value of the referred environment variable. The purpose of this parameter type is being able to embed part of the information about the system configuration inside the individual. This may be handy to avoid freezing that information in the fitness evaluator, or to trace easily which configuration or which machine was able to generate a specific individual.

The syntax for the `environment` type is as follows.

```
<item name="parameter name"
 type="environment"
 variable="variable name"/>
```

Several parameter types are used to express references between graph vertices. References are distinguished between *inner labels*, referring to vertices in the same subgraph, and *outer labels*, that point to the prologue of a different subgraph. They are named *labels* following the convention of assembly languages.

The first label type is the `innerGenericLabel`, that may refer to any vertex in the same subgraph as the one constrained by the current macro. Its description is completed by the `prologue` attribute, that specifies whether the subgraph prologue is a valid target for the reference, the `epilogue` attribute, providing the same specification for the subgraph epilogue, and the `itself` attribute, telling whether the vertex can refer to itself. The allowed values for all these attributes are "true" or "false". All attributes are compulsory.

The corresponding syntax is as follows.

```
<item name="parameter name"
 type="innerGenericLabel"
 prologue="true|false"
 epilogue="true|false"
 itself="true|false"/>
```

The other three are restrictions of the first type. One is the `innerBackwardLabel`, that describes an edge that can only end in a vertex that precedes the one from which it starts. For the `innerBackwardLabel` type only the `prologue` attribute and the `itself` attribute are meaningful. Its syntax is

```
<item name="parameter name"
 type="innerBackwardLabel"
 prologue="true|false"
 itself="true|false"/>
```

The second type is `innerForwardLabel`, that describes an edge that can only go from a vertex to a vertex following it in the subgraph. For the `innerForwardLabel` type the only meaningful attributes are `epilogue` and `itself`. In terms of assembly language, a `innerForwardLabel` is a reference that never forms a loop, since it only corresponds to a forward branch. The syntax is as follows.

```
<item name="parameter name"
 type="innerForwardLabel"
 epilogue="true|false"
 itself="true|false"/>
```

The third, most restricted type is the selfRef type. It describes an edge that always ends in the same vertex from where it starts. None of the other attributes are meaningful for this reference type. In terms of assembly language it corresponds to a code fragment that always refers to its beginning. Its syntax is

```
<item name="parameter name"
 type="selfRef"/>
```

A peculiar form of reference is the uniqueTag parameter type. A unique tag is an identifier guaranteed not to conflict with any other identifier name generated by the evolutionary core. It is considered a reference parameter because its most immediate usage is as a reference inside a single macro. Actually, a vertex in the individual may represent a code fragment containing a small loop. Since labels are always put at the beginning of the phenotype representation of a vertex, a single macro could not describe both the initialization part and the body of a loop. This limitation can be overcome by the use of a uniqueTag parameter, once as a label and a second time as a code reference. Correct usage of the tag inside the macro has to be taken care of by the user, since the core has no way to distinguish whether the tag is used as a label or a reference.

A uniqueTag parameter has no further attributes. Its syntax is

```
<item name="parameter name" type="uniqueTag"/>
```

There is a single type of outer reference, the outerLabel parameter type. An outer label refers to the prologue of a different subgraph. The user can specify several allowed types of subgraph, by listing the subsections that describe them. In this way the corresponding edge in the individual can, in principle, end in the prologue vertex of any subgraph corresponding to one of the listed subsections. If, when the macro is instanced, no subgraph is available, a new one is generated.

The outerLabel type has no further attributes. The allowed subgraphs are listed inside the item element, each one in a ref element. This element, in turn, has two attributes that completely specify a single subsection. These are the section attribute and the subSection attribute. At least one ref element should be specified within the item element. In the ref elements both attributes are compulsory, even if there is a single section in the constraints or a single subsection in the specified section. The syntax is as follows.

```
<item name="parameter name"
 type="outerLabel">
  <ref section="section name" subSection="subsection name"/>
```

```
   . . .
</item>
```

As stated above, it is possible to use a parameter belonging to a type defined at the top level of the constraints library. The type definitions are all contained in the `typeDefinitions` element of the library. The syntax for every type definition is the same as that for the definition of a parameter inside a macro. The only difference is that the definition resides in the `typeDefinitions` element instead that in the macro. The names of the types defined in this way should not conflict with each other.

To use a defined type the parameter should be declared to be of type `definedType`. The `ref` attribute of the parameter, then, contains the name of the type defined globally.

The syntax is as follows: first the parameter type should be defined in the `typeDefinitions` element.

```
<typeDefinitions>
  <item name="type name"
    . . .
  </item>
  . . .
</typeDefinitions>
```

Then the parameter should be defined by referring to the defined type.

```
<item name="parameter name"
  type="definedType"
  ref="type name"/>
```

It should be kept in mind that the `param` element in the expression still has to refer to the *parameter* name, not to the *type* name.

The syntax for the `prologue` and `epilogue` elements is very similar to the syntax for the `macro` element, of which they represent a specialization. The main difference in the syntax of the elements themselves is that the `weight` attribute is meaningless for prologues and epilogues. Indeed, prologues and epilogues are guaranteed to be instanced exactly once for every instance of their containing element.

The other difference is operational, and concerns the use of label parameters. Indeed, using forward labels in an epilogue or backward labels in a prologue is meaningless, and should be avoided, as it could lead to constraints that could never be fulfilled.

Complete examples of constraints libraries can be found in chapter 12.

Chapter 10
Writing a compliant evaluator

Lutter n'est pas avancer.

Boris Vian

During the evaluation phase the μGP core generates the phenotypes of the individuals to evaluate, launches the external evaluator and waits the results.

μGP can generate a set of individuals for evaluation. This is done as a minimal support measure for parallel evaluation. In general the user can configure the tool to evaluate one individual at a time, or more. The specific techniques to actually implement a parallel evaluator are beyond the scope of the book.

In the first case the evaluator can safely assume that only one individual will be available, whereas in the second case nothing should be presumed about the number of indviduals present.

10.1 Information from μGP to the fitness evaluator

Individuals are generated in the form of text files, following the syntactic constraints contained in the constraint library. When used in a Unix-like or Windows environment, these files are written in the current directory.

By default, the name of the fitness evaluator is `./evaluator`, and the name of the individuals is a variation of `individual.input`. Both parameters can be configured, although this is generally more useful for the evaluator name.

The evolutionary core provides information to the evaluator in two explicit and one implicit form. The first is the command line. The evaluator is called, using the defaults as an example, as `./evaluator individual`$\langle name\_1 \rangle$`.input` `...individual`$\langle name\_n \rangle$`.input`. The individuals are listed in the order in which they are generated. The symbols $\langle name\_1 \rangle \ldots \langle name\_n \rangle$ are replaced by the names of the individuals inside the core.

The second explicit form in which the evolutionary core provides information to the evaluator is an additional file containing the names of the individuals to evaluate. Unsurprisingly, this file is named `individualsToEvaluate.txt`. It contains as many rows as the newly generated individuals, each one containing a name.

The implicit information is the content of the directory itself. When the evaluator is invoked, the individuals are already all present in the directory. This information, however, is not always a reliable source to decide which individuals should be evaluated. μGP, in fact, by default deletes the individual phenotypes once they are evaluated, to save space. However, it can be configured so that it never deletes an individual. This option is useful mainly for debug purposes, or to make measurements on the evolutionary process itself.

In addition, the tool can dump all individuals contained in a population prior to evaluation, to cater for cases in which the fitness of an individual depends on the other individuals belonging to the population.

It is important to note that the name of the file in which the fitness should be saved is not provided to the evaluator. By default this name is `individuals.output`, and it also can be configured. The evaluator must possess information on the expected file name.

The default behavior is to evaluate one individual at a time. This allows keeping the evauator simple.

If concurrent evaluation is used, no assumption can be made in advance about the number of individuals generated for evaluation. The only guarantee is that, if the tool has been configured to perform n evaluations in parallel, no more than n individuals at a time will be passed to the evaulator.

First of all, the exact number of individuals generated in the reproduction phase is not known from the start. Second, some individuals can be excluded from the evaluation phase simply because they are clones of other individuals. These two properties of the tool imply that the number of individuals to evaluate at every generation cannot be successfully predicted. At the end of the evaluation phase, then, there will be a remainder of individuals to evaluate, but their number is not predictable.

10.2 Expected fitness format

As seen in previous chapters every individual has a fitness composed of a given number of floating point values. Every fitness can be optionally followed by a comment string, in order to provide more meaningful information to the user.

The expected format for the fitness is rather simple. The evaluator should generate a text file, containing a number of lines equal to the number of individuals to evaluate during a single invocation, each line containing the fitness for an individual.

Every fitness should be composed by a list of positive floating point values, separated by spaces, optionally followed by a string *without spaces*, and terminated by a newline.

If more than one individual has to be evaluated, the fitness values should be output to the file in the same order in which the individuals are passed to the evaluator. Failure to do so would most probably lead to wrong results in the evolution, due to the assignment of the fitness for an individual to a different one. No explicit mapping exists between the names of the individuals and the corresponding fitness values, and no check is possible.

It is also important that fitness for all individuals contain the same number of values, equal to the amount configured at the beginning of the evolutionary run. Otherwise it would not be possible to meaningfully compare two individuals.

In all cases, it is possible to append to the fitness file a special line, that only contains the string "#stop". If this is done the evolutionary core stops evolution at the end of the current generation. This can be useful in case the evaluator detects that the maximum possible fitness has been reached, but this maximum could not be predicted accurately in advance.

10.2.1 Good Examples

The following examples show some possibilities for the fitness file. Provided the tool is configured accordingly, they are correct.

Example: one evaluation at a time, three fitness values per individual, no comment string.

```
2.01 4 1.3e-05
```

Example: one evaluation at a time, two fitness values per individual, with comment string and stop signal.

```
2.01 4 1.3e-05%
#stop
```

In this case the "1.3e-05" is treated as a string. The fact that it also represents a number is totally incidental for the tool, since it expects only two numeric values.

Example: the tool is configured for ten evaluations at a time, but it only generated a set of four individuals. The individuals should receive two fitness values each, and the evaluator generates some coment strings.

```
42.3 96412 ALU:good/CTR:poor
55.2 97218
12.3 99415 ALU:poor/CTR:poor
86.2 96217 CTR:good
```

This example underlines that the comment string is optional for every fitness, not on a global basis. When it exists, the comment string can be of any length.

10.2.2 Bad Examples

The following examples, instead, show incorrect fitness files and possible corrections.

Bad example: the tool is configured for one evaluation at a time, and every individual should get three fitness values.

```
2.01 4 very_good
```

In this case the tool will find only two numeric values, and the string "very_good" cannot be used quantitatively for comparison purposes.

If the phrase "very good", among others, is actually meant to express the third fitness value, it should instead be turned into a numeric mark. For example, a "very bad" result could be expressed as 0, "bad" as 1, and so on, up to "very good".

The corrected example could become

```
2.01 4 5
```

where the "very_good" has been transformed in the 5 mark.

If, instead, the third numeric value is missing because, for this particular individual, it cannot be set meaningfully, the problem is more serious. In this case the user should decide, on the basis of his own understanding of the problem, a conventional value for the third fitness parameter.

Advisable choices change depending on whether such a peculiar individual is to be considered better or worse than normal ones. In the former case, any value greater or equal to the maximum posible value for the third fitness parameter is usable.

The example could then become

```
2.01 4 100.0 very_good
```

but the value for the third fitness parameter strictly depends on the problem.

In the latter case, instead, there is still a choice. A 0 value can be used to express the fact that this individual is worse than any other individual with the other fitness parameters equal. If, however, the user wants to enforce clone extermination, but at the same time wants to make sure that peculiar individuals, although not considered good, are preserved in preference to clones, the third fitness parameter should be set to a value greater than zero but lower than any possible value for normal individuals.

A possibility might be

```
2.01 4 1e-15 very_good
```

with the same warning as above: the actual value needed may change.

If none of these possibilities is viable, because the range for the third fitness parameter actually starts from zero, or if the missing parameter is not the last, the user should seriously consider expressing his problem in a different way.

Bad example: the tool has generated four individuals for evaluation, and expects three finess values per individual.

```
82.3 14.5 96412 ALU:good CTR:poor
55.2 58.4 97218
12.3 99415 ALU:poor/CTR:poor
86.2 -3.57 96217 CTR:good
```

This example contains almost all errors that can be made. The first line is wrong because the comment string contains a space. It is not guaranteed that the tool will work properly after finding such a string. It is, however, guaranteed that the string will not be reported correctly to the user. The third line is wrong because it misses a fitness value. The fourth line is wrong because it contains a negative fitness parameter. The problem with negative fitness parameters is that they would not allow clone extermination to work properly. The only correct line in the file, despite its incomplete appearance, is the second.

One correct alternative might be

```
82.3 14.5 96412 ALU:good/CTR:poor
55.2 58.4 97218
12.3 0.0 99415 ALU:poor/CTR:poor
86.2 0.001 96217 CTR:good
```

Again, the actual choice of the values to use as replacement or in addition depends strictly on the problem, and requires the understanding of the user.

Chapter 11
Implementation details

Not 100% efficient, of course ... but nothing ever is.

Capt. Kirk in *Star Trek*

The μGP approach is centered around the evolutionary core. The tool is composed by about $50,000$ lines of C++ code, comprising 118 classes in 310 files. The project is hosted by Sourceforge on `http://ugp3.sourceforge.net/`.

This chapter describes the most important details about the implementation of the tool. The purpose is providing the user with the information necessary to understand, modify the code, and possibly adapt it to his specific needs.

11.1 Design principles

As described in chapter 3 the entire approach is decomposed in three main blocks. The first is the evolutionary core itself, the second is the constraints library and the third is the fitness evaluator. The μGP tool internally follows this subdivision, and is additionally decomposed.

During design we identified the sections of the tool that were more likely to undergo modification. These sections have been conceptually separated from the rest of the tool. The purpose of the approach is to develop a set of classes that will presumably not require modifications, and use them as a foundation for the rest of the tool.

We anticipated that different users of the tool would want to modify it based on their specific needs. For this reason the code of μGP has been written keeping a clear separation between its concepts and functions. Ideally, for every desired modification, it should be clear what part of the code has to be changed.

We decided to structure the tool as a series of libraries, each of which provides services at a single level. This choice has the main purpose of making the different parts reusable in different projects without the need to operate on the code. At the same time, the subdivision of the tool in different modules, with clearly defined interfaces, allows modifying each part of the code almost independently from the rest.

11.2 Architectural choices

Apart from the main decomposition of the entire approach, the tool is subdivided in different levels. The basic concept is to make each level provide a foundation for the upper levels. At the same time, it is desirable that each level is only used by the level directly above it, avoiding dependencies of the high-level code on the details of the lowest-level libraries. This also includes the dependence on the interface of the library. In this way, ideally, every module only depends on a limited set of interfaces, and these too may be redefined without completely disrupting the architecture.

At the lowest level lies the code that handles the constraints for the evolutionary core. This choice may look counter-intuitive, but the constraints are only stored as a descriptive entity. This means that they can be used by other code, but do not depend on the fact that they will be applied to graphs. Constraints are kept in their tree form, and checks for compliance are performed elsewhere. The classes that store and manipulate the constraints, as well as reading them from the XML library file, form the *Constraints* library.

The Constraints library is unlikely to need modifications in order to extend its functionality. If the user really needs to extend the syntactic possibilities of the library, he may probably obtain the same effect by manipulating the individual in the fitness evaluator, before actual evaluation.

In a different set of classes the basic data structures for individual representation are managed, providing a foundation to store and manipulate graphs and the information associated to tags. The classes at this level form the *Graph* library. It provides a foundation for all other evolutionary modules.

It is worthwhile to note that this library is not, strictly speaking, an evolutionary library. It is a library that allows building, copying and generically manipulating graphs. It also allows attaching information to graph vertices, and subjecting the graph to constraints.

Upon this layer, the concept of individual is built. This includes the addition of the concept of fitness to the constrained tagged graph. Individuals can be compared to decide which one is better, whereas two graphs could only be compared for equality.

Individuals are organized in populations, and manipulated through genetic operators. They are selected for reproduction and evaluated. All these activities, and several other support ones, are taken care of by the *Evolutionary Core* library.

Its classes perform the bulk of the work needed for actual evolution.

The highest level configuration of the evolutionary process is performed in the front end module. This includes deciding how many populations are cultivated during the run and the type of each population, parsing the command line arguments and the configuration files, setting up the default parameters.

11.2.1 The Graph library

The Graph library fulfills two distinct roles. The first is allowing basic manipulation of the basic data structures that describe the evolved entities. The second is providing the tools needed to enforce compliance of the evolved individuals with the constraints.

Vertices and edges

The most basic class in the library is the Edge class. It simply represents an edge between two graph vertices. It can have tags, but these are not used to represent the relation between the two vertices. Tags are only used during manipulation of the constrained graph, when the edge is detached from its destination vertex and might be reattached either to the same vertex or to a different one.

The Edge class provides basic methods to create an edge, set its destination, get its source or destination. Additionally, it allows to read its description from an XML document or write it to a file.

The Node class represents the vertices of the graph. As for the Edge class, it can have tags, but they are not necessary to represent the graph. Every vertex has an unique id string.

The Node class allows attaching edges starting from or ending in the specified vertex, detaching and destroying edges starting from or ending in the vertex, checking if the vertex is connected with a specified edge, getting the number of edges starting from or ending in the vertex, selecting one of them by numeric index. Additionally, it allows to read its description from an XML document, and to write an XML description to a file.

The Tag class, although seemingly strictly connected to the Edge and Node classes, actually belongs to a different library, the *shared* library. This choice underlines the very generic nature of a tag, that may be attached to generic entities inside a program.

The CNode class, finally, references the constraint library. Its purpose is the description of a "constrained vertex", that is a vertex belonging to a constrained graph. Whereas the Node class could be used to describe generic graphs, the CNode class possesses information about the expected structure of a subgraph. Therefore, it uses the special next and prev tag names to identify edges connected to the corresponding vertices of the subgraph, and the place tag to track the position of each vertex inside the subgraph sequence. It also provides methods to know whether a given vertex represents a prologue or an epilogue of the containing subgraph, of a graph or of the entire individual. In addition, it provides methods to detach it partially or completely from the containing subgraph and to follow, forwards or backwards, the linear structure of the subgraph. Since it references a constraint the CNode class also provides methods to randomly populate one or more parameters, to validate the content of parameters against the constraint and to generate the external representation of the vertex.

Subgraphs and graphs

Vertices are organized in subgraphs. Starting from the first vertex of a subgraph,
a path connecting it to the last subgraph vertex is guaranteed to exist in a valid
individual. This path can be thought of as a skeleton for the subgraph: its main purpose is to knit together the subgraph vertices, imposing a well-defined order relation
among them. The linear structure of the subgraph originally copied the sequential
order of instructions in a program, and it has been preserved as it greatly simplifies
housekeeping operations.

Subgraphs are materialized by the CSubGraph class. There is no Subgraph
class, because its generic properties have been factored in two different classes. The
CSubGraph class refers to the constraints library. It has knowledge of the expected
structure for a subgraph, in particular about the minimum and maximum number of
vertices inside a given subgraph.

The CSubGraph class provides methods to get and set the prologue and epilogue,
to validate the subgraph, to check whether a vertex precedes or follows another
vertex, and to reconstitute a valid subgraph in case it is modified and some edges
remain floating.

Several actual operations on the subgraph are executed via the Slice class. It
can be seen as an array of vertices with some operations added. Every subgraph is
composed of a prologue and an epilogue vertices and a slice. Operations available
on a slice are appending a vertex, swapping a vertex pair, inserting another slice at
a defined position, removing a part of the slice from a given position, reversing the
order of a part of the slice. These operations have been chosen partly as a minimal
interface to perform every possible manipulation on a subgraph, partly as an imita-
tion of mutation mechanisms actually occurring in DNA. The Slice class does not
refer to the constraints library, so it cannot perform validation or manipulation of
the *contents* of the subgraph. It is, instead, the workhorse of *structure* manipulation
for a subgraph.

It is appropriate to mention here the NodeContainer class. It is the base class
for constrained subgraphs, graphs and graph containers. It is the class that represents an entity with a prologue and an epilogue vertices. This structure is used for
all parts of an individual. The NodeContainer class has no information about the
structure (or even the existence) of the other vertices that constitute the graph. Instead, it represents the structural relationships of the various parts of the individual through a parent-son relation. Every NodeContainer object can have another
NodeContainer as its parent.

Subgraphs are collated together in graphs. The generic Graph class keeps information about the vertices in the graph, but not of the subgraphs. The reason for this
is that the subdivision of graphs into subgraphs is closely related to the constraints
for the individuals, whereas the Graph class is meant as a generic graph representation. The Graph class provides basic manipulation of the graph. It allows creating a
graph, empty or from a file description, adding a vertex, removing a vertex, adding
an edge between two vertices, counting the vertices or referring to one by index. It

should be noted that the order of vertices inside the Graph class is not necessarily related to the order in the subgraphs.

The class that explicitly refers to the subgraphs is the CGraph class. It provides methods to add or remove a subgraph, to replace a subgraph with a different one, to refer to a specific subgraph or vertex, to count subgraphs.

CGraph also refers to the constraints, allowing to validate the graph. This class materializes the concept of *constrained tagged graph* as depicted in chapter 3. In a graph subgraphs are kept in the same order in which they have been added to the graph. This is the same order in which they are generated in the external representation.

Graphs are ultimately stored in graph containers to form the genotype of an individual. As stated in chapter 3 individuals are composed of sets of graphs. These are managed through the CGraphContainer class. This class provides methods to inquire for a specific constrained vertex or graph, to duplicate the container, to add a constrained graph to the set. In addition, it allows operations useful to manipulate an individual, as getting a randomly chosen subgraph, generating a random set of graph that complies with the constraints, validating the graph set.

The Graph library is not expected to need extensive revision by the user, since it provides very basic representation, manipulation and validation operations. It is useful to understand its basic classes in order to delve into the details of the Evolutionary Core library, since this library relies on the details of individual representation to perform its actions.

11.2.2 The Evolutionary Core library

The Evolutionary Core library is involved in all aspects of the evolutionary process. At the most basic level, it provides a graph set with its meaning as an individual, by associating it with a fitness and a population. It is in charge of handling fitness evaluation, including the support for parallel evaluation. It provides the concept of population, keeping track of the associated parameters and maintaining the statistics of the evolution. Last but not least, it provides all of the genetic operators applied during a run.

Individuals

One of the most basic classes in the Evolutionary Core library is the Individual class. Its main purpose is to provide a graph set, which would otherwise be just a data structure, its meaning as an individual. Every individual belongs to a population, and cannot persist outside it. Also, each individual is associated with a fitness. These two properties constitute the main difference between a graph container and an individual.

The `Individual` class also supports additional features. Each individual has a birth instant, measured in generations since the beginning of evolution, a projected death instant, and an age, measured in generations.

An individual can also keep track of its parents and the genetic operator by which it has been generated. This can useful to track the descent of a given individual across generations, as well as to tune the activation probabilities for operators.

The base `Individual` class is actually not used on its own. Instead, it is the superclass for `EnhancedIndividual` and `MOIndividual`.

The enhanced individual, materialized by the class `EnhancedIndividual`, adds three main features to the base individual. The simplest is the explicit handling of the concept of *elite*. Depending on the evolution parameters and the ranking (past and present) of the individual inside its population, its age may not be equal to the difference between the current generation and the birth instant. As long as the individual belongs to the elite its age does not increase with generations.

The second feature is the use of a modified fitness, named `EnhancedFitness`. The purpose for this modified fitness is making clone scaling easier. As described in chapter 4, individuals exactly identical to others already existing in a population can have their fitness values scaled down by a factor that depends on how many clones are contained in the population. This is implemented by actually associating every individual with two fitnesses. The first is the *measured* fitness, as is reported by the external evaluator, whereas the second is the *scaled* fitness, computed internally. Ranking of individuals inside a population is based on scaled, not measured, fitness. The two fitnesses are coupled in the `EnhancedFitness`. This class also takes into account the so called *clone count*, that is the number of clones of a given individual that exist in the population with an higher rank. If an individual has just been inserted in the population, meaning that it has just been generated, its clone count is the number of clones among the μ regular individuals of the population plus the number of clones that have been generated during the current application of genetic operators. In case of twin clones, therefore, those generated later are scaled more than the earlier ones. In general, older clones are favored against younger ones. This is made to avoid that individuals may achieve a sort of immortality by propagating in the population as recurring clones.

Finally, the `EnhancedIndividual` keeps a record of its own contribution to population entropy, in the form of a delta entropy value. This is the difference between the entropy of the complete population and the entropy of the same population, from which the considered individual has been removed.

The enhanced individual is used instead of the simple individual since its features, in most cases, significantly enhance the efficiency of the evolutionary process.

The `MOIndividual` materializes the concept of *multi-objective individual*. It is an individual whose fitness is to be used for true multi-objective optimization. Differently from simple and enhanced fitness, the components of a multi-objective fitness have no priority over each other. Instead, they have all the same importance. The most direct implication is that fitness values do not belong to an ordered set. Two fitness may be equal, may *dominate* each other, meaning that all the components of one fitness are greater or equal to the corresponding components of the other, or they may be simply not comparable. The class that materializes the concept of multi-objective fitness, named MOFitness, extends EnhancedFitness. Clone scaling is a capability of MOIndividual from the start, as the MOIndividual derives from the EnhancedIndividual.

Populations

As already stated above, individuals in μGP cannot exist outside of a population, materialized by the Population class. As with the simple individual the simple population is used as a base class for the sake of performance.

In the μGP a population is not a passive container for individuals, as several details of the evolutionary process are delegated to the Population class and its subclasses. Every population is associated with the set of individuals contained in it, and with the set of parameters for that population.

Population parameters include population size μ, the number λ of genetic operators applied per generation, the initial size ν for population, the set of operator activation probabilities, operator strength σ, the maximum number of generations for the process, the self-adaptation inertia α, the cardinality of the set of fitness values.

The Population class contains methods to update the self-adaptive parameters, to increase the age of individuals, to compute some statistics about the evolution. It also provides methods to perform a single evolution step, to add existing individuals to the population or to merge an additional entire population to an existing one, to associate a genetic operator to the population, to check for stop conditions. It also acts as an interface by specifying several methods that derived classes must implement.

As is the case with simple individuals, a simple population is not used directly, but only as a base class for more advanced population types. To take full advantage of enhanced individuals they are collected in a special population type, unsurprisingly named EnhancedPopulation. This class keeps track of which individuals are clones of others, of the overall population entropy, of the maximum attained fitness and of the number of idle generations (generations during which no improvement in the best fitness is observed).

The EnhancedPopulation class implements several methods defined as pure virtual in Population. The most important of these are those to create a random individual, to perform the survival phase, to self-adapt the parameters, to evaluate all individuals, to compare two individuals for ranking purposes.

Evolution performed using the EnhancedPopulation class is effectively single-objective, even if the fitness components are multiple. If different goals are expressed using fitness components the first one dominates all the others, and any improvement in the first component, however small, is preferred to improvements in subsequent components. In an enhanced population individuals are ranked linearly in a total order relation. The whole population may be seen as a list of individuals, starting from the fittest and sloping down to the worst surviving one.

When the user wants to optimize several metrics, possibly accepting a trade-off between them, the fitness components should not dominate one another. Furthermore, it is perfectly acceptable that individuals represent different alternatives, among which no single best solution can be picked up. One usual approach, employed in μGP, is to divide the population in levels. The first, topmost level is composed by all individuals that are not dominated by any other individual. The second level is then composed by all individuals that are dominated only by individuals in the first level, and so on for all lower levels.

The class responsible for managing the population as a set of individuals grouped in levels is MOPopulation. This class does not extend EnhancedPopulation the same way as MOIndividual extends EnhancedIndividual. Instead, it directly extends Population. The class MOPopulation stores information about which individuals are clones of others, population entropy, the number of levels in the population and about the number of idle generations.

MOPopulation implements the same virtual methods of the Population class as EnhancedPopulation does.

In an ideal multi-objective setup, all individuals in the same level are ranked equally. This happens during the reproduction phase, but for the purposes of the survival phase it is not always possible to treat all the individuals equally, even if they belong to the same level. There is a finite amount of space in the population, and a level may have to be cut to preserve population size. This means that the MOPopulation class must be able to force a ranking inside a level, to decide which individuals will survive and which will not.

To this end a measure of perceived strength is performed on every individual. This is based on the comparison of an individual fitness with the fitness of every other individual. An ordering between any two individuals is forced by first comparing levels, then the perceived strengths, then the contribution of the individual to population entropy, and finally the birth instant. The first of these comparisons that does not yield an equality result determines the total outcome.

The population is not simply cut at the last level after imposing a total ordering, however. Instead, the survival phase is performed using a reverse tournament selection, with the same τ parameter as for the tournament selection in the reproduction phase. In this case the tournament is reversed in the sense that τ individuals are randomly chosen, and then the *worst* one is discarded. The reverse tournament selection is only performed among individuals in the last level. As a result, after the survival phase, the multi-objective population contains the best levels plus a stochastic selection of the last one.

Genetic operators

Regardless the population type and number, and also regardless of the type of individuals, the low-level work of evolution is performed by genetic operators. The μGP uses three main types of operators: mutation operators, recombination operators and local search operators. The genetic operators used in the μGP do not depend on the type of individual on which they act. Indeed, all operators are defined to manipulate objects of the Individual class, and are applicable to all subclasses.

Genetic operators need to be registered before they can be used. This is done before the actual evolution takes place. The authors expect the addition of custom operators to be the most common modification that users may perform on the code. Since new classes and object are not automatically detected in a C++ runtime environment the registration is needed to provide a uniform and flexible mechanism for addition and deletion of operators.

All operators are derived from a common class, called GeneticOperator. This class defines the common interface for all operators, including the method for generating offspring and a method that returns the number of parents that an operator expect to be provided as input.

The GeneticOperator class, in addition, is in charge of managing thee registration process, and provides static methods to register an operator, to search for an operator by index number or by name, and to unregister them all after evolution is complete.

Many operators may need to manipulate individuals in the same way, for example they may need to insert a vertex in the graph, or they may need removing one. Some basic methods for manipulation are provided by the class OperatorToolbox. A specific operator toolbox is defined for every individual that has to be modified, binding it to its CGraphContainer composing class. An operator toolbox provides random navigation in a graph container, random insertion and random deletion operations.

There are a number of predefined genetic operators in μGP, listed below. Currently three recombination operators, eight mutation operators and three local search operators are defined.

An important concept is that any operator may fail generating offspring. This follows from the fact that new individuals must comply with the constraints. It may not always be possible to apply an operator without breaking them, so every operator has to contemplate the chance of failure. All operators, in one form or another, have to check the validity of the generated offspring, and discard it if necessary.

Recombination operators imply the exchange of genetic material between individuals to generate offspring. This cannot be done in an arbitrary way, since the offspring must be valid individuals. To ensure that generated individuals are correct (or, at least, to avoid cases in which they would certainly be wrong) the exchange is only performed between *compatible subgraphs*. Two subgraphs are compatible if and only if they refer to the same subsection and the same section of the constraints. For instance, the constraints may define a subsection containing some raw data, and another subsection specifying operations to perform on those data. By limiting genetic exchange to corresponding subsections a garbling of data and operations is avoided.

OnePointSafeSimpleCrossoverOperator is the simplest recombination operator. Given two parents, it selects a random subgraph from the first one, then searches for a compatible subgraph in the second one. Once two suitable subgraphs are found, a single cut point is chosen for each one, and two offspring are generated in which the second part of the chosen subgraphs are exchanged. This is done regardless whether any vertices in the swapped sections are connected to other subgraphs, so a final validation step is performed to ensure that correct individuals are generated.

OnePointSafeCrossoverOperator is similar to the operator above, but it also transfers any subgraph referred to by the vertices in the swapped sections. The extra effort is justified for individuals with a complex structure, whereas it is useless when individuals have a linear structure with just one subsection in the constraints. Transferring a subgraph means copying it from one individual to the other. If the copied subgraph is no longer referred to in the source individual then it is deleted.

TwoPointSafeSimpleCrossoverOperator is the last recombination operator. It selects a random subgraph from the first parent, chooses a compatible subgraph in the second one, then locates two cut points within each subgraph. It generates two offspring in which the parts between the two cut points are swapped, transferring also any subgraph referred to by the vertices being moved.

Mutation operators can be classified in two orthogonal ways. The first is about whether they certainly change the size of the individual or not, the second relates to the object they act upon, be it a single vertex or an entire subgraph. Being orthogonal, the two classifications define four groups of operators. Mutation operators exist for all these groups.

All mutation operators use the concept of strength. After one application, the operator is repeatedly applied again with a probability equal to the strength. The greater the strength, the larger th eaverage number of times the operator is applied for a single offspring.

InsertionMutationOperator changes the size of an individual adding a random vertex to the graph. The reader should note that if the constraints dictate that the added vertex refers to a different subgraph (it contains an OuterLabel parameter), it is connected to an existing subgraph of the same type. If no suitable subgraph exists in the individual, the insertion fails.

RemovalMutationOperator also changes the size of an individual removing a random vertex from the graph. If the removed vertex was connected to a different subgraph, that subgraph may become an unconnected component of the graph.

ReplacementMutationOperator does not change the size of the individual. It substitutes a random verrtex of the graph with a random one, subject to the condition that it refers to the constraints in the same subsection as the original vertex. The parameters of the verteex are also chosen randomly.

AlterationMutationOperator is similar to the previous one, save that it does not change the vertex type. It chooses a random vertex in the graph and sets all parameters to random values.

SingleParameterAlterationMutationOperator is an even more restricted mutation operator. It sets to a random value a single parameter in a randomly chosen vertex.

SubGraphInsertionMutationOperator again changes the size of an individual adding a subgraph to the graph. All vertices in the new subgraph are chosen randomly, and have random parameters. If a vertex in the new subgraph has to connect to another subgraph, a compatible subgraph is chosen, if it exists, otherwise the operator fails.

SubGraphRemovalMutationOperator chooses a random subgraph from the indivdual and removes it. All edges starting from inside that subgraph and ending in a different subgraph are removed. If a vertex in another subgraph refers to the subgraph being removed the edge is connected to a subgraph of the same type. If no other compatible subgraph exists the operator fails.

SubGraphReplacementMutationOperator may change the size of an individual. It randomly selects a subgraph and replaces it with a new one, composed of randomly chosen vertices.

Local search operators perform an exploration of some *neighborhoood* of a given individual. Currently the neighborhood is defined as the set of individuals that differ from the first one for the value of a single parameter. The parameter can be any ranged parameter, and is the same for all the neighborhood. A ranged parameter is a parameter that can have a value between a minimum and a maximum. Structural parameters (labels), constant parameters or environment parameters are not considered for exploration. For instance, if an individual contains a parameter that can have 10 different values, the associated neighborhood contains 9 individuals.

The term local search refers to the fact that the exploration is done only within this neighborhood. Local search operators differ from mutation operators because all offspring belong to the neighborhood defined above, whereas mutation operators may modify different parts of the same individual.

ScanMutationOperator is conceptually the simplest search operator. Given an individual, it chooses a single numerable parameter and produces a child individual for every possible value of the parameter.

LocalScanMutationOperator explores the neighborhood at increasing distances from the source individual. It uses the concept of strength, and is reapplied with probability equal to the strength. The first time it generates offspring at unit distance from the source individual, and every time it is reapplied it generates offspring at increasing distances.

RandomWalkMutationOperator also uses strength, but operates differently. Given a source individual, and a single ranged parameter in that individual, it generates offspring using a normal distribution for that parameter. The strength is used both as the standard deviation and as the probability of reapplying the operator.

Evolutionary algorithm

In the same way as many individuals can be instantiated within a population, several populations can be exist in a single evolutionary algorithm. The class that materializes the evolutionary scheme is EvolutionaryAlgorithm. This class provides methods to add populations to the algorithm, to run it, to save the status to file and to recover an existing evolutionary algorithm from file.

The class also contains a protected method to perform a single step of the algorithm. This method does little more than calling the corresponding method on every population that has not already ended its evolution.

11.2.3 Front end

The top level of the μGP code is the front end. Although logically and physically distinct from the rest of the code, the front end is not a proper library. Rather, it sits on top of all the other libraries to compose a usable program.

The most important class in the front end is Program. It loads the settings file, sets up the loggers, initializes the evolutionary algorithm and finally starts it.

11.3 Code organization and class model

As stated above, the code is organized into libraries, except for the front end. Two of these libraries have been described, but they do not end up the μGP executable. A total of six libraries, plus the front end, compose the code. Every library is contained in a directory of the same name in the distribution, much akin to a package in Java programming.

Shared is a low-level library. It contains several classes and interfaces used in different contexts. These classes are collected together since they provide services that are largely independent of the application domain. For instance, they manage things like command-line options, environment variables, tags, the definition of settings options, unlimited counters, and so on. All these concepts are widely used elsewhere in the code, but they might be implemented in the same way for very different applications. A special mention is due to the exceptions, defined as subclasses of the Exception class and further collected in the Shared/Exceptions directory.

Log is a second low-level library. It is in charge of generating all the output directed to the user. This includes all messages on the console, and all information or debug files requested by the user. However, it neither generates the XML representation of the algorithm status, nor the statistics files. The genotype to phenotype mapping is also outside the scope of the library.

XmlParser is a generic open-source library (TinyXML) for the construction and parsing of a document tree from the XML source. Further discussion of this library is outside the scope of the book. The library is available from http://sourceforge.net/projects/tinyxml/

Constraints is the library devoted to the handling of the syntactic constraints of the indivduals. Its classes materialize the concepts of sections, subsections, macros and parameters. It depends on the application domain, indeed it gives the μGP the ability to transform genotype data into a file with a defined syntax.

Graph is the middle-level library. It manipulates graphs, subgraphs and vertices, allowing the transformations needed for evolution. It does not strictly depend on the application domain. In fact, it is possible to use the Graph library for deterministic transformations. However, it is not a complete graph library, since several common algorithms (say, the Minimum Spanning Tree) would be of little use in the tool.

EvolutionaryCore is a high-level library. It sits on top of the other libraries, actually performing the evolution. By definition, it depends strictly on the application domain of the tool.

Graph and EvolutionaryCore are discussed in more detail in sections 11.2.1 and 11.2.2.

The front end is not actually a library, but it too is packaged in a directory inside the distribution.

Libraries are compiled as regular object files and statically linked. This increases the executable size but promotes portability across platforms.

A number of classes in the Shared, EvolutionaryCore, Graph and Constraints libraries implement the XML interface defined by the abstract class XMLIFace, contained in the Shared library. This interface specifies three methods. The writeXml() method serializes the object in XML format to an output stream, readXml() deserializes it from an XML element, and finally getXmlName() returns the XML element name for the class. Most classes that implement this interface do not actually implement those methods in the regular .cc file, but in a separate .xml.cc file. This approach is meant to limit the scope of modifications to the code in case the user wants to use a different XML parsing library.

Some simplified class diagrams are presented below to help clarify the code organization. No complete class diagram is reported, as it would be unintelligible. Rather, the class diagrams below focus on particular parts of the tool, detailing parts that the user may want to modify.

The class diagrams are simplified in several ways. They include only classes strictly involved in the particular aspect analyzed, and also omit attributes and methods of the classes that are not necessary for understanding. To preserve legibility of the diagrams the method and attribute signatures are omitted.

A significant amount of code, present in μGP, is not described to avoid confusion and cluttering. Getter and setter methods are almost always omitted from descriptions and class diagrams, as they are often quite trivial. Also, methods that implement the XML interface of a class are frequently absent from the diagram, as well as methods that override inherited ones. Finally, when a class overloads a method or a constructor, it is only reported one time in the diagram, as it would make little sense to have the very same line two or more times in a diagram.

Figure 11.1 depicts the organization of classes that handle the individuals. The main purpose of the Individual class is to act as a unifying framework of every concept related to a single individual. It logically includes the individual genotype, the genotype-phenotype mapping and the resulting fitness.

The Individual class is seldom used *as is*, since only its subclasses are actually instanced. Every individual is uniquely tagged by the id attribute. The birth, death and mAge attributes track the anagraphic data of the individual, taking into

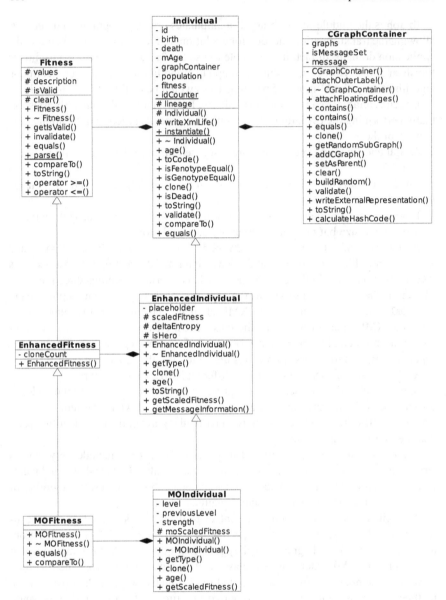

Fig. 11.1 Simplified class diagram: Individual

account its permanence in the elite in case that applies. The association attributes graphContainer and fitness keep track of the components of the individual, whereas the population attribute links it upwards to its enclosing poplation.

Important methods include age(), that increases the current age of the indi-vidual and, if it is too old, decrees its death, toCode(), that writes the external representation of an individual to a file, `validate()`, that checks that the individual complies with its constraints.

One key method is `instantiate()`, defined statically and overloaded one time. This method is used, when deserializing an entire population, to construct an individual before its contents are actually known. In case the user wants to add new types of individul, he has to add the relevant code to the `instantiate(const string&, const Population&)` method.

The `EnhancedIndividual` class is associated to `EnhancedFitness` by the `scaledFitness` attribute. In `EnhancedIndividual` the `placeholder` attribute is used as a performance aid when searching for clones.

The `age()` method is redefined since it has to take into account the possibility that the individual is part of the elite. The `getMessageInformation()` method is instrumental in entropy and delta-entropy computation.

Similarly, the `MOIndividual` class is associated to `MOFitness` using the `moScaledFitness` attribute. In `MOIndividual` the `level` attribute tracks the current Pareto level of the individual. The `previousLevel` attribute allows discovering whether an individual in the Pareto front has been dominated by another one in the last generation. In this case the count of generations without fitness improvements is reset to zero. The `strength` attribute measures the perceived strength of an individual with respect to all the other individuals in the population. This strength is used, when needed, to discriminate individuals within a single Pareto level.

The actual content of the individual is stored in a `CGraphContainer` class. Derived classes for the individual use this content through the base `Individual` class. We consider the constrained tagged graph to be general enough not to need modifications when used to represent different types of individuals. Inheritance for the fitness, instead, exactly follows that of the individual. Classes for the individual are derived in chain, and every type of individual has a corresponding class for the fitness, with the same derivation sequence.

In the `MOFitness` class the `compareTo()` method overrides the corresponding method from `Fitness`. This is necessary because the regular fitness or the enhanced fitness allow total ordering, whereas the multi-objective fitness does not, so it must contemplate the possibility that two fitness values are not comparable.

Figure 11.2 reports the simplified class diagram for the `Graph` library. The reader can see that several relationships occur among all the classes included in the diagram, and these do not always follow the inheritance chains.

The classes shown can be divided in three rough categories. The first is a set of classes that represent generic concepts, like graphs, vertices and edges, that may apply to any tool. These are the `Edge`, `Node` and `Graph` classes. The second is a set of classes specific to μGP, that represent concepts related to the constrained tagged graph. These are the `CNode`, `CSubGraph`, `CGraph`, `ConstrainedElement` and `NodeContainer` classes. The third, only containing the `Slice` class, is the set of classes that are used for optimization purposes. The slice is not a basic concept, but rather a convenient way of treating a subgraph. It is a linear representation of a subgraph, starting from the first vertex after the prologue and terminating at the last

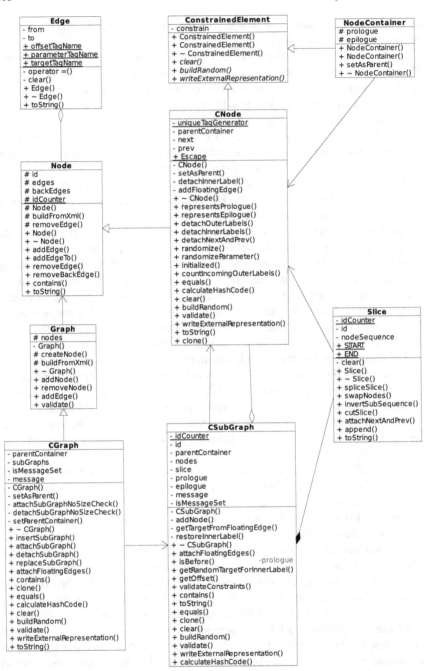

Fig. 11.2 Simplified class diagram: Constrained Tagged Graph

vertex before the epilogue. The order of the vertices in the slice is the same in which they can be visited following the next reference of each.

For performance reasons the CSubGraph class uses the Slice as a component, and at the same time it keeps track of its CNode constituents through a map. The slice is especially useful in applying the crossover operators.

Fig. 11.3 Simplified class diagram: Evolutionary Operators

Figure 11.3 depicts the relationship between the genetic operators. Methods have been omitted in all but one operator class, since they have essentially identical names and perform conceptually identical functions.

The GeneticOperator class represents the unifying concept of a genetic operator. This class is also responsible for the housekeeping operations involving the genetic operators. These include registering the operators, unregistering them, selecting an operator for application, releasing the memory taken up by invalid individuals. It also declares the abstract method `generate()`, whih actually applies the genetic operator to a set of input individuals.

Two abstract classes extend the `GeneticOperator` superclass. These are `MutationOperator` and `CrossoverOperator`. The first is the base class for all mutation operators, that is all operators that receive a single genotype as input and generate one or more offspring from it. The second is the base for all operators that recombine genetic material from two parents to generate offspring.

We advise the user wanting to introduce genetic operators that recombine genetic material from three or more parents to derive a further class from `GeneticOperator`, to factor all common methods of actual operators.

The classes derived from `MutationOperator` and `CrossoverOperator` are the actual genetic operators used by μGP. All of them define a constructor and three methods. These are the `getName()`, `getAcronym()` and `generate()` methods. The first two just return human-readable text to describe the operator, the last performs the offspring generation.

The scheme for `generate()` is always the same: the parent individuals are copied using the `clone()` method of `Individual`, then the copies obtained are manipulated to obtain the new individuals. The rest of μGP expects that the parents never change. If this happens, wrong results are almost guaranteed.

The last class visible in the diagram is `OperatorToolbox`. To avoid unnecessary cluttering its relations with other classes are not displayed, but it is actually used by all operators. As the name suggests, it is a collection of methods to manipulate the genetic material. We think that this class is the right place to define new generic manipulation methods that the user may want to introduce.

Figure 11.4 shows the overall archtecture of the evolutionary algorithm. The unifying class here is `EvolutionaryAlgorithm`. For every evolutionary run only one instance of this class exists. The evolutionary algrithm comprises one or more populations. The concept of population is materialized by the `Population` class. Actual populations can only be of `EnhancedPopulation` or `MOPopulation` type.

Every population is associated with a corresponding set of parameters. This correspondence is not only a one-to-one association, but it is also a type correspondence. Every population of a given type has parameters of a corresponding type. An enhanced population has parameters of `EnhancedPopulationParameters` type, whereas parameters of type `MOPopulationParameters` correspond to a multi-objective population. The type hierarchy is the same for populations and population parameters. We advise users wanting to add new population types to follow the same scheme, in order to maintain a tight control on the code. If a new population type is desired, it should be complemented with a corresponding individual type (see figure 11.1), fitness type and parameters type.

Independently of its type, every population is associated, through the parameters, to both a fitness evaluator and a statistics class. The `FitnessEvaluator` class represents the external evaluator and takes care of the evaluation operations, including setting the evaluation queue, running the external program, collecting the fitness values, deleting the individuals already evaluated if so required, signaling a possible stop request by the evaluator.

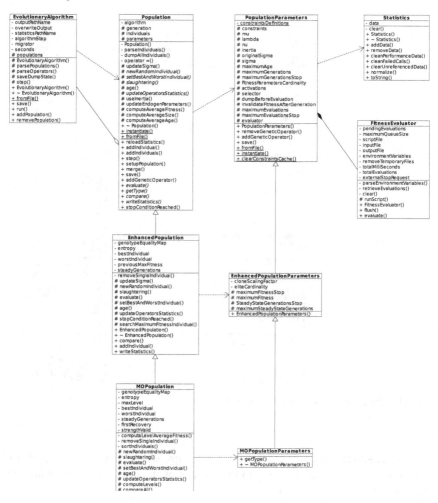

Fig. 11.4 Simplified class diagram: Evolutionary Algorithm

Since fitness evaluation is a generic activity, that does not depend on the structure of a population or the representation of an individual, the `FitnessEvaluator` class does not have any subclasses.

Figure 11.5 depicts the organization of the program front end. The `Program` class is responsible for initialization activities, including reading the command line arguments, setting up the logs, instancing the evolutionary algorithm. The `Program` class contains a settings class, `MicroGPSettings`, that is responsible for reading the initial settings file and initializing the general parameters.

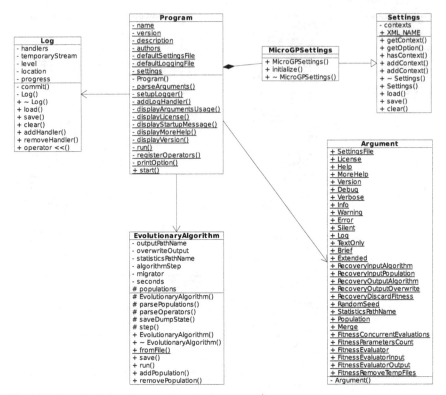

Fig. 11.5 Simplified class diagram: Front End

MicroGPSettings is a subclass of Settings, whose responsibility is that of providing a hierarchical structure to the settings, with contexts, options within the contexts and argument values.

The Argument class contains all possible command line arguments as static strings. It is not the responsibility of Argument to hold the value of a command line argument, but only to provide the argument names, so its constructor is made private.

μGP has a comprehensive log system, useful for both debugging and tracking of the evolutionary process. The central clas of this system is Log.

The log architecture includes four general concepts. These are the message record, handling of the communication channel, formatting of the message, and level of the message.

The Record class holds a message record. Besides the message itself, a record contains information aboout the message level, the instant in which it has been generated, the code location that produced it, and whether it contains progress information. The latter indication is important because typically messages about operation progress are meant to superimpose each other, and not to be saved individually.

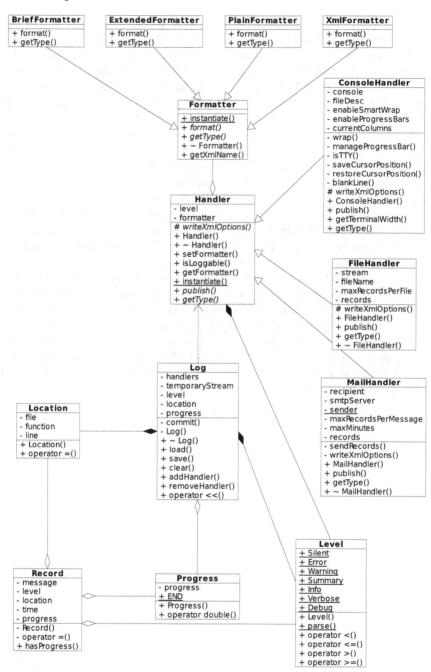

Fig. 11.6 Simplified class diagram: Logging system

Progress information, like a progress bar or a completion percentage, may be important at the time when it is generated, but is almost meaningless later.

The handling concept is materialized by the Handler class. It is the base class for a number of specialized handlers whose responsibility is to correctly forward messages to different channels. In version 3.2 the Handler class has three subclasses, ConsoleHandler, FileHandler and MailHandler. These forward messages respectively to a command line terminal, to a file or to a SMTP server.

Related to, but independent from the concept of channel handling, is the concept of message formatting. In this context the term formatting is used to indicate the type and amount of information that is conveyed with each message. For instance, it indicates whether a timestamp is included in each message, or whether messages are generated in XML format. The Formatter class represents the generic concept of message formatting. It is the base class for the BriefFormatter, PlainFormatter, ExtendedFormatter and XmlFormatter classes. Each of these classes defines its own format() method, that transforms each record message in a message string ready to be sent to an output channel.

Every message has an associated verbosity level. Messages with an high verbosity level are transmitted to the user only if a log exists with a verbosity level equal or higher. If the verbosity of a log is lower, the message is not transmitted through that log. Very important messages, therefore, have a very low level.

In addition, for debugging purposes, the log system includes the Location class, whose purpose is to hold the exact location in the code where a message is generated. In this way it is easier to pinpoint the code that produces an unexpected message, and find possible bugs.

Chapter 12
Examples and applications

> *Human beings, who are almost unique in having the ability to learn from the experience of others, are also remarkable for their apparent disinclination to do so.*
>
> Douglas Adams

This chapter contains a number of examples to illustrate the use of μGP. In the following each example is described completely, so that each experiment can be easily repeated. Every section contains detailed information about the preparation of the settings file, of the population settings file and of the constraints file. In addition, it contains the code of the fitness evaluator. The results of the evolutionary runs are provided for each experience.

The examples are not chosen for their usefulness, but rather to bring out some difficulties that may arise in the use of any evolutionary tool, and to show how these can be solved using μGP. For instance, in some cases the user may need to design the constraints file and the fitness evaluator together to correctly describe individuals whose syntactic structure does not match trivially the structure of the constraints file. In other cases describing the individuals is not a problem, but their semantic may be, such as when it contemplates the possibility of endless loops. Sometimes the simplest possible fitness function may be too difficult to optimize, or it may lead to bloating. In such cases the user may have to modify the fitness function, or to add further fitness values.

At the same time, the results allow the reader to appreciate the way in which the different parameters influence the evolutionary process. The performance of the tool may be sensitive to different parameters when confronted with different problems. In this perspective, the following examples are meant to provide an insight on the evolutionary process.

12.1 Classical one-max

This problem is somewhat like a "hello world" of optimizing methods in general, and of evolutionary algorithms in particular. The problem is simple. Let's call s a generic string of bit. Given the set S_N of all the possible strings of bits of length N, the goal is finding a string $s_m \in S_N$ so that the number of bits set to '1' in the string is maximum.

The problem has an immediate solution, represented by a string made of N '1' bits. Obviously, this problem does not require an optimizer, but can be used as a test to check that an optimizer actually works.

12.1.1 Fitness evaluator

Despite the simplicity of the problem there is stil ample choice for the implementation of the fitness evaluator. The simplest choice is a program that takes a string of '0' and '1' as input and produces as output the number of '1' characters in the string.

One source of problems with this approach is the ability of μGP to produce variable-size individuals. The result of the evolution would then be different from expectations, since the evoutionay core would be able to increase the fitness of individuals just by adding random bits to their genome. On average, one half of those bits would be '1', so the fitness could increase without bounds. There would be no selective pressure on the individuals for shedding the '0' bits.

There is a simple route for solving this problem. Just assign zero fitness to all individuals that have a number of bits different from N. This approach works, and eventually leads to the expected result.

The same result could be obtained by choosing which genetic operators are used during evolution. If all operators that could change the size of the individual are suppressed by setting their weight to 0, and the initial size of the individuals is set to N, then all individuals generated would be the right size, and then would be no need to check it.

What's wrong with this approach? Nothing, but the user should be careful, because it relies on *a priori* knowledge of the problem domain. In particular, it is known that a sequence of alteration mutations, local mutations and scan mutations can lead to the desired result, no matter what the starting point is. If such knowledge is available it is perfectly acceptable to use it. When this approach can be used, it may lead to substantial savings in optimization time, since it greatly restricts the search space.

For other problems, allowing the individuals to grow or shrink outside the problem domain may make alternative evolutionary routes available and allow the optimizer to reach an optimal solution.

The example provided with the tool uses the approach described above. Individuals are bound to be exactly N bits long, and every mutation that changes the size results in a failure. No individual longer or shorter than N is ever evaluated, so the evaluation script does not check the size.

Below is the evaluation script.

```perl
#!/usr/bin/perl -w-

# Starting from v3.1.2_1142 fitness scripts can use
```

```
# (again) environment variables:
#
# $UGP3_FITNESS_FILE : the file created by the
#                      evaluator
# $UGP3_OFFSPRING    : the individuals to be
#                      evaluated
#                      (space separated list)
# $UGP3_GENERATION   : generation number
# $UGP3_VERSION      : current ugp3 version.
#                      eg. 3.1.2_1142
# $UGP3_TAGLINE      : full ugp3 tagline.
#                      eg. ugp3 (MicroGP++)
#                      v3.1.2_1142 "Bluebell"

open OUT, ">$ENV{UGP3_FITNESS_FILE}"
  or die "Can't create $ENV{UGP3_FITNESS_FILE}: $!";
foreach $file (@ARGV) {
    open F, $file or die "Can't open $file: $!";
# read a single line from file F
    $_ = <F>;
# count the '1' characters
    $n = tr/1/1/;

# the comment string is the current time
    $time = localtime;
    $time =~ tr/ /_/;
    print OUT "$n $file\@$time\n";
}

close OUT;
```

The fitness script is written in PERL scripting language. A modified version, with additional comments, is reported here. First it opens the fitness file for writing, or aborts if it is unable to do that. In case the fitness script aborts without generating any file, the whole evolutionary process will be aborted.

Then the script parses its command line arguments. Every argument is the name of an individual to evaluate. Again, if opening the corresponding file is not possible, the evaluation is aborted.

Every file is expected to contain a single line, which is read and scanned to count the '1' in it. No attempt is made to count the total number of characters in the line.

The comment string is set to the name of the individual followed by the time of evaluation, with the spaces replaced by underscores.

This script is able to evaluate many individuals, as specified by the concurrent evaluations parameter in the population settings file, but evaluation is actually sequential. To achieve actual concurrent evaluation the script should be modified so that it sets up all the needed processes or threads. Even if evaluation is not parallel it may still pay off to evaluate many individuals together, since it will save several calls to the perl interpreter, with the corresponding initialization sequences.

12.1.2 Constraints

The constraints for one-max are conceptually simple. Every individual must be composed by a linear sequence of N character, either '0' or '1'. Global and section prologues and epilogues are not needed.

Constraints are reported in a modified form to fit the page, splitting long lines in shorter ones. Splitting the lines, especially quoted strings, would raise an error in an actual run.

```xml
<?xml version="1.0" encoding="utf-8"?>
<?xml-stylesheet type="text/xsl"
  href="http://www.cad.polito.it/ugp3/transforms/
              constraintsScripted.xslt"?>
<constraints
  xmlns="http://www.cad.polito.it/ugp3/schemas/
              constraints"
  id="One-Max"
  xmlns:xsi="http://www.w3.org/2001/XMLSchema-instance"
  xsi:schemaLocation="http://www.cad.polito.it/ugp3/
                          schemas/constraints
                      http://www.cad.polito.it/ugp3/
                          schemas/constraints.xsd">
  <typeDefinitions>
    <item xsi:type="constant" name="bit_type">
      <value>0</value>
      <value>1</value>
    </item>
  </typeDefinitions>
  <commentFormat><value/></commentFormat>
  <identifierFormat>n<value /></identifierFormat>
  <labelFormat><value/>: </labelFormat>
  <uniqueTagFormat><value /></uniqueTagFormat>
  <prologue id="globalPrologue"/>
  <epilogue id="globalEpilogue"/>
  <sections>
    <section id="bitString"
            prologueEpilogueCompulsory="false">
      <prologue id="sectionPrologue"/>
      <epilogue id="sectionEpilogue">
```

```
          <expression></expression>
        </epilogue>
        <subSections>
          <subSection id="main" maxOccurs="1"
                        minOccurs="1" maxReferences="0">
            <prologue id="stringPrologue"/>
            <epilogue id="stringEpilogue"/>
            <macros maxOccurs="50" minOccurs="50"
                    averageOccurs="50" sigma="10">
              <macro id="bitString">
                <expression><param ref="bit"/>
                </expression>
                <parameters>
                  <item xsi:type="definedType"
                        ref="bit_type" name="bit" />
                </parameters>
              </macro>
            </macros>
          </subSection>
        </subSections>
      </section>
    </sections>
  </constraints>
```

The constraints contain an empty global prologue and epilogue, and a single section. In the section appear an empty prologue, an epilogue with an empty expression and a single subsection. It is interesting to note that the empty prologue and the epilogue with an empty expression produce the same effect, that is no string is produced at the beginning or at the end of an individual.

The subsection, named "main", can occur exactly one time and cannot be referenced. In this specific case specifying the allowed number of references has no meaning, since there is no macro in the constraints with a reference.

Again, the subsection has empty prologue and epilogue. After that, the constraints specify that the subsection can contain from a minimum of 50 to a maximum of 50 macros, with the same average. This just means that the number of macros is fixed, and individuals with a different number of vertices in the corresponding subgraph are not valid and will not be evaluated. The non zero sigma parameter is actually meaningless, all individuals are generated with the specified number of vertices.

There is only one type of macro in the constraints, in which the expression is an unadorned parameter of type bit_type, defined at the start of the constraints as either '0' or '1'.

12.1.3 Population settings

The population parameters for this example are reported below. All options, including optional ones, are used. As for the constraints, some elements are reported split on two or more lines to fit the page.

```xml
<?xml version="1.0" encoding="utf-8" ?>
<parameters type="enhanced">
  <cloneScalingFactor value="0"/>
  <eliteSize value="0"/>
  <maximumFitness value="50"/>
  <maximumSteadyStateGenerations value="20"/>
  <mu value="10"/>
  <nu value="10"/>
  <lambda value="10"/>
  <inertia value="0.9"/>
  <fitnessParameters value="1"/>
  <maximumAge value="10"/>
  <sigma value="0.9"/>
  <invalidateFitnessAfterGeneration value="0"/>
  <constraints value="onemax.constraints.xml"/>
  <maximumGenerations value="100"/>
  <maximumEvaluations value="1000"/>
  <selection type="tournamentWithFitnessHole" tau="1"
             tauMin="1" tauMax="1" fitnessHole="0" />
  <evaluation>
    <concurrentEvaluations value="4" />
    <removeTempFiles value="true" />
    <evaluatorPathName
        value="./onemax.fitness-script.pl" />
    <evaluatorInputPathName value="individual.in" />
    <evaluatorOutputPathName value="fitness.out" />
  </evaluation>
  <operatorsStatistics>
    <operator ref="onePointSafeCrossover">
      <weight current="1" minimum="0" maximum="1"/>
    </operator>
    <operator ref="onePointSafeSimpleCrossover">
      <weight current="1" minimum="0" maximum="1"/>
    </operator>
    <operator ref="twoPointSafeSimpleCrossover">
      <weight current="1" minimum="0" maximum="1"/>
    </operator>
    <operator ref="singleParameterAlterationMutation">
      <weight current="1" minimum="0" maximum="1"/>
```

```
      </operator>
      <operator ref="insertionMutation">
        <weight current="1" minimum="0" maximum="1"/>
      </operator>
      <operator ref="removalMutation">
        <weight current="1" minimum="0" maximum="1"/>
      </operator>
      <operator ref="replacementMutation">
        <weight current="1" minimum="0" maximum="1"/>
      </operator>
      <operator ref="alterationMutation">
        <weight current="1" minimum="0" maximum="1"/>
      </operator>
      <operator ref="subGraphInsertionMutation">
        <weight current="1" minimum="0" maximum="1"/>
      </operator>
      <operator ref="subGraphRemovalMutation">
        <weight current="1" minimum="0" maximum="1"/>
      </operator>
      <operator ref="scanMutation">
        <weight current="1" minimum="0" maximum="1"/>
      </operator>
      <operator ref="subGraphReplacementMutation">
        <weight current="1" minimum="0" maximum="1"/>
      </operator>
      <operator ref="randomWalkMutation">
        <weight current="1" minimum="0" maximum="1"/>
      </operator>
      <operator ref="localScanMutation">
        <weight current="1" minimum="0" maximum="1"/>
      </operator>
    </operatorsStatistics>
</parameters>
```

An enhanced population is used, with 10 individuals. At each generation, 10 genetic operators are applied. The entropy fitness hole is not used and the parameters of `tournamentSelection` are set to choose an individual only, thus performing a simple random selection on the individuals each time a genetic operator is applied.

All operator weigths are equal, exactly as they are generated using the `ugp3-population` tool.

The evolution is stopped as soon as it reaches the maximum possible fitness value, or if 20 generations are elapsed without any progress in the best fitness value. This event is extremely improbable, unless the population parameters are changed to extreme values.

12.1.4 µGP settings

Below are reported the general tool settings for one-max. As usual, some options are split on different lines to fit the page. We recommend that in actual use they are kept on single lines.

These are actually fairly standard settings. Apart from the reference to the population parameters file, nearly identical settings may be used for a wide range of problems.

```xml
<?xml version="1.0" encoding="utf-8" ?>
<settings>
  <context name="evolution">
    <option name ="populations">
      <population name="OneMax-Population"
          value="onemax.population.settings.xml" />
    </option>
    <option name="statisticsPathName"
          value="statistics.xml" />
  </context>
  <context name="recovery">
    <option name="recoveryInput" value="" />
    <option name="recoveryInputPopulations" value="" />
    <option name="recoveryOutput" value="status.xml" />
    <option name="recoveryOverwriteOutput"
          value="true" />
    <option name="recoveryDiscardFitness"
          value="true" />
  </context>
  <context name="logging">
    <option name="std::cout" value="info; brief" />
  </context>
</settings>
```

These settings specify a single population, described by the parameters in section 12.1.3. No recovery input is specified, and the recovery output file is overwritten at every generation. The settings also specify to discard the fitness values of the recovered status, but since there is no recovered status, this option has no effect.

No seed for the random number generator is specified. Should the user desire to repeat a series of identical runs, the randomSeed element in the evolution context should be set to a specific value.

The logging is kept brief. Only the standard output is generated, and no file is written. Given the purpose of the example, logging should only be activated if the user suspects the presence of a software bug.

12.1.5 Running

Once the files described above are ready and placed in the same folder, the evolution can start by simply invoking the μGP executable, ugp3, without any command-line parameter. Evolution should end after a few seconds, finding the optimal solution.

The user can verify that the optimal solution has been reached by using the μGP extractor software. Provided that the μGP settings file is exactly as reported above, typing ugp3-extractor status.xml on the console will generate a text file containing the best individual, compute its fitness and display a brief report of the operations executed. We recommend the user to take note of these names, as they may be easily overlooked in a directory with many files inside. If a first run does not return the optimal solution, a new run most likely will. If the tool is regularly unable to find the best solution, chances are that the settings files are not conform to the samples reported above: and the user should thus check their correctness.

A first rule of thumb is that the maximum number of generations should be in linear relation with the size of the population. A safe bet is to allow at least $2n$ generations in a run with n individuals.

The user could also check that the genetic operators are not deactivated: any operator that does not appear in the population settings file or has a weight of zero, is not used. If several operators are missing from the settings or have a weight of zero, it might be impossible to perform the optimization at all.

On the other hand, choosing which operators are used may help speed up the evolution. Some operators do not change the size of the individual, some may or may not change it, some will certainly grow or shrink the individual. Removing the latter from the list of available operators should speed up evolution, simply because more valid individuals will be produced per generation.

A quick demonstration the user may perform consists of running the evolutionary process both with the settings described above and with modified population settings. The modified settings will prescribe a weight of zero for the insertion mutation, removal mutation, all subgraph mutation operators. These are all operators that are guaranteed to fail, since the individuals have a fixed size and only a single subgraph, as by constraint settings. The operators are deactivated by setting the current weight to 0. Operators with a current weight of zero will not be used, their success rate will not be positive, thus their weight will not change.

We tried the experiment repeating the run 1000 times for each setting, without controlling the seed of the random number generator. This means that the results are not exactly repeatable. Your mileage *will* vary.

With the first setup we obtained the optimal solution 999 times out of 1000, on average in about 26.9 generations. The second setup found the optimal solution in each run, with an average of generations 25 generations elapsed. If you choose to use self adaptation of μGP parameters, eventually genetic operators that fail too much will see their activation probability decrease to minimum levels. This procedure speeds up the evolution, *de facto* removing useless operators.

12.2 Values of parameters and their influence on the evolution: Arithmetic expressions

Arithmetic functions are often used as test benches to evaluate the convergence and performance of evolutionary algorithms. Some of them are well known in literature, for example all tests developed by Kenneth De Jong, but in principle every function with specific features (e.g. a great number of local optima and a single global optimum) can be used for this purpose.

In all the cases presented in this section, choosing the fitness function and the representation of the individuals is trivial: the fitness is obtained directly from the arithmetic function and each individual is an array of real numbers in a given interval.

More interesting are the variation of the performance of μGP obtained by tweaking the population parameters. It will be shown how each parameter influences a run and thus it should be set to an appropriate value in every experiment in order to maximize the performance of the evolutionary algorithm.

12.2.1 De Jong 3

The third function developed by De Jong is defined as follows:

$$f_{DJ3}(x) = 5 \cdot n + \sum_{i=1}^{n} \lfloor x \rfloor, \qquad x_i \in [-5.12, 5.12] \qquad (12.1)$$

The function is monomodal and not continouos, and it has an infinite number of local minima $f(x^*) = 0$ for $x_i^* \in [-5.12, -5]$, with $i = 1, 2, ..., n$.

For the following experiments $n = 5$, so each individual is composed by 5 real numbers, $x_{1,...,5} \in [-5.12, 5.12]$. Some parameters, summarized in Table 12.1 and Table 12.2 are not changed through all the experiments.

Parameter	Value
μ	1 000
ν	500
λ	250
σ	0.970, 0.980
MaximumAge	20
maximumSteadyStateGenerations	5 000
maximumGenerations	10 000
Seed	5987579

Table 12.1 Parameters of all the following experiments.

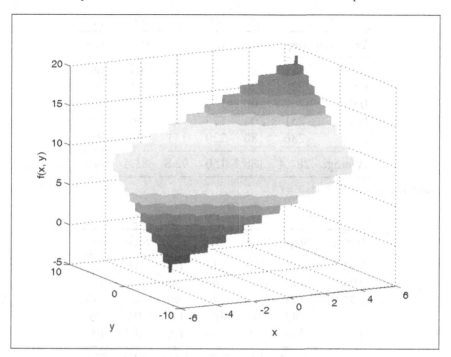

Fig. 12.1 De Jong's third function

Operator	Curr. Probability	Min. Probability	Max. Probability
replacementMutation	0.5	0	1
singleParameterAlterationMutation	0.5	0	1

Table 12.2 Genetic operators used in the experience

12.2.1.1 The τ parameter

The τ parameter describes the number of individuals that will be randomly selected to take part in the tournament selection to choose the parents for an activated genetic operator. Incresing τ makes the choice more deterministic, steadily rewarding individuals with better fitness values, while decreasing τ makes the choice of the parents more and more random.

Thus, τ should be chosen wisely, depending on the function you are trying to optimize. As a rule of thumb, high values of τ are beneficial up to a certain point, where the trend becomes the opposite. In Table 12.3 to Table 12.8 we see how τ tweaking works for this particular arithmetic function, with different values of the EliteSize and Inertia parameters. For each combination of values, the number of steps μGP required to find the global optimum is listed.

In the third De Jong function, an increase in τ leads to a small improvement, up to $\tau = 128$, then the system has a small setback and there are no further improvements. Fig. 12.2 summarizes the results.

$\tau = 8$		16	32	64	128	256
Inertia	Steps	steps	steps	Steps	Steps	Steps
0.93	322	180	92	72	64	69
0.94	296	170	94	90	61	65
0.95	267	206	169	95	82	109
0.96	251	204	175	96	96	85
0.97	286	180	220	111	104	103
Average	284.4	188	150	92.8	81.4	86.2

Table 12.3 Results for EliteSize = 8

$\tau = 8$		16	32	64	128	256
Inertia	Steps	Steps	Steps	Steps	Steps	Steps
0.93	224	157	114	105	64	69
0.94	149	92	76	90	61	65
0.95	305	177	146	95	82	116
0.96	298	210	163	118	96	85
0.97	256	239	177	195	104	103
Average	246.4	175	135.2	120.6	81.4	87.6

Table 12.4 Results for EliteSize = 16

$\tau = 8$		16	32	64	128	256
Inertia	Steps	Steps	Steps	Steps	Steps	Steps
0.93	276	154	114	72	64	69
0.94	281	145	76	90	61	65
0.95	272	163	169	112	82	116
0.96	360	184	172	111	96	85
0.97	290	263	187	156	104	103
Average	295.8	181.8	143.6	108.2	81.4	87.6

Table 12.5 Results for EliteSize = 32

12.2.1.2 The ν parameter

The ν parameter describes the initial size of the first population, containing only randomly-generated individuals. In some experiments, exspecially those where the evaluation of a single individual takes some time, it can be useful to draw upon an initially larger quantity of genetic material. Aside from these specific cases, how-

$\tau = 8$		16	32	64	128	256
Inertia	Steps	Steps	Steps	Steps	Steps	Steps
0.93	268	160	110	72	64	69
0.94	269	150	76	90	61	65
0.95	186	188	134	112	82	116
0.96	289	175	145	111	96	85
0.97	227	255	182	174	104	103
Average	247.8	185.6	129.4	111.8	81.4	87.6

Table 12.6 Results for EliteSize = 64

$\tau = 8$		16	32	64	128	256
Inertia	Steps	Steps	Steps	Steps	Steps	Steps
0.93	229	171	110	72	64	69
0.94	251	150	76	90	61	65
0.95	282	186	134	112	82	116
0.96	303	201	145	111	96	85
0.97	354	226	174	174	104	103
Average	283.8	186.8	127.8	111.8	81.4	87.6

Table 12.7 Results for EliteSize = 128

$\tau = 8$		16	32	64	128	256
Inertia	Steps	Steps	Steps	Steps	Steps	Steps
0.93	229	160	110	72	64	69
0.94	255	150	76	90	61	65
0.95	236	176	134	112	82	116
0.96	284	224	145	111	96	85
0.97	228	163	174	174	104	103
Media	246.4	174.6	127.8	111.8	81.4	87.6

Table 12.8 Results for EliteSize = 256

ever, it is expected that any initial advantage v can provide to the fitness values in the population will be lost as the generations go on.

For the third function of De Jong, the latter proves true: as shown in Fig. 12.3, any initial increase in the average fitness value is rapidly lost, and the graph assumes a similar shape no matter the value of v in the experiment.

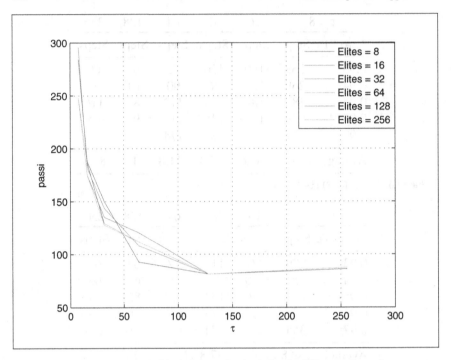

Fig. 12.2 Number of steps needed to find the optimal solution for different values of τ.

12.2.1.3 The FitnessHole parameter

FitnessHole is a parameter that can be extremely useful in experiments where individuals have distinct blocks (e.g. individuals that describe several assembly functions), since certain values help to reward individuals with a pattern which is uncommon in the population at a given generation. That increments entropy in the system and preserves some potentially useful genetic material that could otherwise be wasted.

In functions where an individual is basically an array of numbers, however, the same values for this parameter can be a disadvantage: lacking distinct blocks, the only result of tweaking FitnessHole will be a random selection of individuals during a tournament.

As shown in Fig. 12.4, this is the case with the third De Jong function. FitnessHole should be altered from its default value of 0 only when the structure of a single individual is really complex.

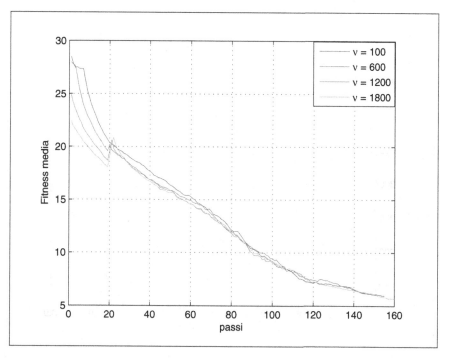

Fig. 12.3 Influence of v on the average fitness for each generation.

12.2.2 De Jong 4 - Modified

The fourth function chosen by De Jong to be included in his *test suite* provides a good example for parameter tweaking. In the original function, the random variable η has a gaussian distribution $N(0, 1)$; in this experiment, however, the function has been slightly modified. η, in fact, is considered having a uniform distribution $\in [0,1)$, because in its original version, the fourth De Jong function does not have a global minimum. To increase the difficulty of the problem, η is included in the sum. Thus, μGP is requested to minimize 30 random variables while simultaneously searching for the minumum of a function with 30 variables.

$$f_{DJ4}(x) = \sum_{i=1}^{30} (i \cdot x_i^4 + \eta), \qquad x_i \in [-1.28, 1.28] \qquad (12.2)$$

The global minimum is:

$$f_{DJ4}(x^*) = 0 \quad for \quad x^* = (0, 0, ..., 0). \qquad (12.3)$$

While locating the zone near the minimum is trival, finding the exact global optimum is difficult. In that zone the random component η is in the same order of magnitude of $\sum_{i=1}^{30} i \cdot x_i^4$, so fitness values oscillate in the range $(0, 1)$. Selection and

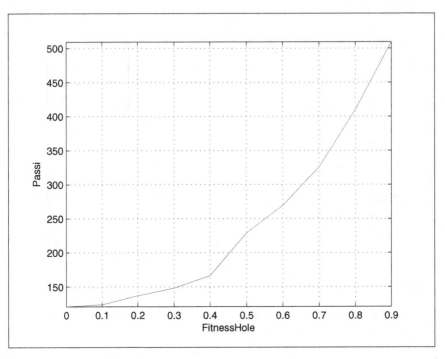

Fig. 12.4 Influence of `FitnessHole` on the number of steps needed to converge.

reproduction of individuals are thus strongly influenced by the constantly changing environment. An appropriate choice of μ and λ parameters can help the convergence even in this hard situation.

12.2.2.1 The μ and λ parameters

Finding the ideal value of μ and λ is a problem-specific issue. In the results of a series of experiments reported in Fig. 12.6, we can notice how the number of generation steps decreases rapidly for increasing values of λ. The number of evaluations, however, drops to a minimum and then slowly climbs up: the correct value for λ should always be chosen in conjuction with the value for μ.

12.2.3 Carrom

The complex Carrom function shows how some genetic operators provided with μGP can significatively improve the behavior of the evolutionary algorithm. The function is also known as *Carrom table* and is defined by the subsequent equation:

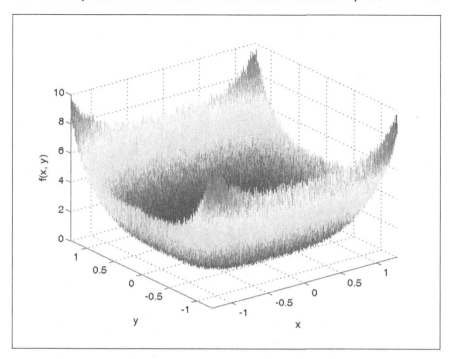

Fig. 12.5 Fourth De Jong function.

$$f(x) = -\frac{1}{30} \left\{ \cos(x_1)\cos(x_2)\exp\left[\left|1 - \frac{(x_1^2 + x_2^2)^{\frac{1}{2}}}{\pi}\right|\right] \right\}^2 \qquad (12.4)$$

The function is multimodal and it has four points of global minimum in the domain $x_i \in [-10, 10]$ with $i = 1, 2$ of value $f(x^*) \simeq -24.1568155$. The cartesian coordinates that identify the four points are $x^* = (x_1, x_2) \simeq (\pm 9.6463, \pm 9.6463)$.

12.2.3.1 Preliminary run

In a preliminary series of runs, μGP is tested against the Carrom function with two different set of parameters, differing mainly for the population size. The objective is to provide the reader with statistics on the convergence when only two basic genetic operators are used. Parameters used can be found in Table 12.9 and Table 12.10. Table 12.11 reports the results of this first series of experiments.

The great number of evolutionary steps needed to find the solution are a clear indication of the complexity of the problem. Among the two sets of runs, experiment 2 presents slightly better results, probably because of the more favorable ratio $\frac{\tau}{\mu}$.

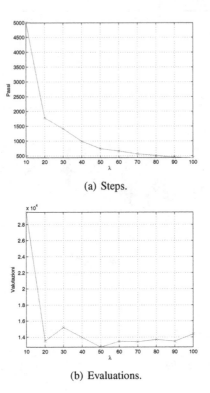

(a) Steps.

(b) Evaluations.

Fig. 12.6 Variation of parameter λ.

	Experiment 1	Experiment 2
Parameter	Value	Value
μ	100	300
ν	50	100
λ	33	33
σ	0.929	0.929
maximumSteadyStateGenerations	5000	5000
MaximumAge	20	20
EliteSize	2	2
$\tau = \tau_{min} = \tau_{max}$	64	64
ε	0.000001	0.000001
Seed	5987579	5987579

Table 12.9 Preliminary experiment. Population parameters.

12.2.3.2 Improvements with genetic operators

The behavior of μGP is then observed during the course of four different series of runs, each one with a different set of genetic operators. The initial activation probability of each operator is equal.

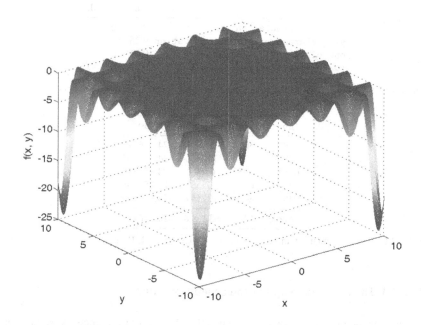

Fig. 12.7 Carrom function

Operator	Curr.	Min.	Max.
replacementMutation	0.5	0	1
singleParameterAlterationMutation	0.5	0	1

Table 12.10 Preliminary experiment. Genetic operators.

	Experiment 1			Experiment 2		
Inertia	Steps	Evaluations	Best Individual	Steps	Evaluations	Best
0.900	8783	145988	-24.156808	7339	135021	-24.156758
0.910	9922	166216	-24.156815	10420	174602	-24.156805
0.920	9972	155432	-24.156813	7338	130522	-24.156811
0.930	8915	145645	-24.156814	6839	124357	-24.156808
0.940	10990	176858	-24.156814	10398	171328	-24.156795
Average	9716.4	158027.8	-24.156813	8466.8	147166	-24.156795

Table 12.11 Preliminary experiment. Results.

The first experiment introduces two *crossover* genetic operators, *onePointSafeSimpleCrossover* and *twoPointSafeSimpleCrossover*. The complete list of genetic operators used is in Table 12.12. The results in Table 12.13 show a clear improvement: the duration of a single run decreases by about 30%, while the number of individuals evaluated drops to a 50%.

Operator	Curr.	Min.	Max.
replacementMutation	0.25	0	1
singleParameterAlterationMutation	0.25	0	1
onePointSafeSimpleCrossover	0.25	0	1
twoPointSafeSimpleCrossover	0.25	0	1

Table 12.12 Improvements with genetic operators, experiment 1. Genetic operators.

Inertia	Steps	Evaluations	Best
0.900	5014	55948	-24.156815
0.910	6778	110320	-24.156793
0.920	5955	67093	-24.156815
0.930	6239	105589	-24.156768
0.940	8474	127544	-24.156799
Average	6492	93298.8	-24.156798

Table 12.13 Improvements with genetic operators, experiment 1. Results.

12.2.3.3 The alterationMutation **genetic operator**

Not all genetic operators, however, are beneficial to the convergence a specific problem: the user should always take care when choosing the operators to include. Some of them may actually worsen the performance of μGP, because they are not able to work on the structure of the individual. For example, *alterationMutation* changes a number of different nodes in the individual with random values: but it fails if the node has no parameters. In the structure of our individual, both the prologue and the epilogue are empty macros with no parameters, so the operators fails often. The great number of failures of *alterationMutation* has direct repercussion on the steps needed to reach an optimal solution. Operators used in this test are presented in Table 12.14, while the results are in Table 12.15.

Operatore	Curr.	Min.	Max.
replacementMutation	0.2	0	1
singleParameterAlterationMutation	0.2	0	1
alterationMutation	0.2	0	1
onePointSafeSimpleCrossover	0.2	0	1
twoPointSafeSimpleCrossover	0.2	0	1

Table 12.14 *alterationMutation*, experiment 2. Genetic operators.

Inertia	Steps	Evaluations	Best
0.900	10182	148224	-24.156811
0.910	10203	145705	-24.156807
0.920	5780	98916	-24.156739
0.930	10492	148785	-24.156815
0.940	7708	118161	-24.156814
Average	8873	131958.2	-24.1567972

Table 12.15 *alterationMutation*, experiment 2. Results.

12.2.3.4 The `randomWalk` genetic operator

randomWalk is one of the genetic operators unique to μGP: basically, it is used to introduce more determinsm into individual creation, thus helping the algorithm to reach an optimal solution in all problems where at least a part of the fitness landscape can be explored effectively by a hill-climber algorithm. *randomWalk* proves its efficacy in this problem, cutting the time needed to reach the optimal solution by an order of magnitude, as shown in Table 12.17. In Table 12.16 all the operators used in this test.

Operatore	Curr.	Min.	Max.
replacementMutation	0.166	0	1
singleParameterAlterationMutation	0.166	0	1
alterationMutation	0.166	0	1
onePointSafeSimpleCrossover	0.166	0	1
twoPointSafeSimpleCrossover	0.166	0	1
randomWalkMutation	0.166	0	1

Table 12.16 *randomWalk*, experiment 3. Genetic operators.

Inertia	Steps	Evaluations	Best
0.900	127	4185	-24.156816
0.910	135	4206	-24.156815
0.920	147	4474	-24.156815
0.930	161	4939	-24.156815
0.940	134	4216	-24.156815
Average	140.8	4404	-24.1568152

Table 12.17 *randomWalk*, experiment 3. Results.

scanMutation is the equivalent of *randomWalk* for integer parameters. It has the same behavior, but it should be used in problems where the macros composing an individual present a great number of integer parameters.

12.3 Complex individuals' structures and evaluation: Bit-counting in Assembly

While arithmetic functions are useful to quickly identify the long-term and short-term effects of population parameters on the evolution, the examples reported in 12.2 share a common, trivial structure of the individuals. To explore some of the expressive potential of μGP constraints file, nothing is better than code generation, a task which the first version of the evolutionary algorithm was developed to tackle.

The aim of this experiment is to make μGP evolve an assembly function able to correctly count the number of bits set to 1 in the integer passed as an argument to the function. Not only the representation of individuals is not as intuitive as it would be in an arithmetic function, but the evaluator is not provided and needs to be conceived with care to effectively solve the problem.

12.3.1 Assembly individuals representation

The first thing that comes to mind when thinking about assembly are the single instructions. μGP provides a powerful mean to define a type of parameter that assumes a finite number of fixed values, TypeDefinitions.

```
<typeDefinitions>
  <item xsi:type="constant" name="register">
    <value>%eax</value>
    <value>%ebx</value>
    <value>%ecx</value>
    <value>%edx</value>
  </item>
  <item xsi:type="constant" name="instruction">
    <value>addl</value>
    <value>subl</value>
    <value>movl</value>
    <value>andl</value>
    <value>orl</value>
    <value>xorl</value>
    <value>test</value>
    <value>cmp</value>
  </item>
  <item xsi:type="constant" name="branch">
    <value>ja</value>
    <value>jz</value>
    <value>jnz</value>
    <value>je</value>
    <value>jne</value>
```

```
        <value>jc</value>
        <value>jnc</value>
        <value>jo</value>
        <value>jno</value>
    </item>
</typeDefinitions>
```

It can be easily noticed in code above that not all the instructions have been included in the same `item`. This is a choice, to easily define different macros with different kinds or number of arguments (e.g., all instructions in `item` *instruction* have two parameters, while all instructions in *branch* only take one parameter). It is also useful to create an `item` for register names, since they will be extensively used in the macros.

The prologue of our individual will be a series of fixed assembly commands common to all functions: values stored in some registers are saved, then the integer passed to the function is put into register `%eax`. The same holds true for the epilogue: a series of fixed commands that return the result to the calling function and restore the initial values in the registers.

```
        <prologue id="sectionPrologue">
            <expression>
.globl foo
            .type    foo, @function
foo:
            pushl    %ebp
            movl     %esp, %ebp
            subl     $4, %esp
            movl     8(%ebp), %eax
            movb     %al, -4(%ebp)
            pushl    %ebx
            pushl    %ecx
            pushl    %edx
            </expression>
        </prologue>
        <epilogue id="sectionEpilogue">
            <expression>
            popl     %edx
            popl     %ecx
            popl     %ebx
            leave
            ret
            .size    foo, .-foo
            </expression>
        </epilogue>
```

The macros, on the other hand, need to express all possible assembly instructions. The macros chosen are reported in the code below. `instrDirectDirect` represents

all the instructions with two register as parameters, while `instrConstDirect`
expresses those instructions which have a register and an integer as parameters.
`branchCond` describes all instruction that jump to a label. Notice that the argument
here is a label that refers to a specific line in the individual, and will be automatically
created by μGP when individuals are instantiated.

```
<macros maxOccurs="infinity" minOccurs="1"
                  averageOccurs="70" sigma="60">
  <macro id="instrDirectDirect">
    <expression>  <param ref="ins"/>
                  <param ref="sreg"/>,
                  <param ref="dreg"/>
    </expression>
    <parameters>
      <item xsi:type="definedType" ref="instruction"
            name="ins" />
      <item xsi:type="definedType" ref="register"
            name="sreg" />
      <item xsi:type="definedType" ref="register"
            name="dreg" />
    </parameters>
  </macro>
  <macro id="instrConstDirect">
    <expression>  <param ref="ins"/>
                  $<param ref="scon"/>,
                  <param ref="dreg"/>
    </expression>
    <parameters>
      <item xsi:type="definedType" ref="instruction"
            name="ins" />
      <item xsi:type="integer" base="dec" minimum="0"
            maximum="255" name="scon" />
      <item xsi:type="definedType" ref="register"
            name="dreg" />
    </parameters>
  </macro>
  <macro id="branchCond">
    <expression>  <param ref="ins"/>
                  <param ref="target"/>
    </expression>
    <parameters>
      <item xsi:type="definedType" ref="branch"
            name="ins" />
      <item xsi:type="innerGenericLabel" name="target"
            itself="true" prologue="true"
```

```
            epilogue="true"/>
    </parameters>
   </macro>
</macros>
```

12.3.2 Evaluator

The evaluator for this particular experiment needs to be designed with the final objective in mind. It is important to provide μGP with a fitness landscape as smooth as possible. The evaluator is composed by two parts:

- A main function written in C;
- A script that compiles an assembly file with the main and runs it.

```
FITNESS\_FILE=fitness.output
rm -f foo fitness.error.log \$FITNESS\_FILE
gcc -o foo main.o \$1 -lm 2\>fitness.error.log
./foo 2\>fitness.error.log \>\$FITNESS\_FILE
if [ -s fitness.error.log ]; then
    echo \"0\" \> \$FITNESS\_FILE
    date \>\> error.log
    more fitness.error.log \>\> error.log
fi
```

Each individual is passed to the evaluator as an argument: the evaluator compiles it with the main in C and runs the resulting executable. As it is clear by the code reported above, the program calls the assembly function generated by μGP with a range of different integers, rewarding the individual if it computes correctly the number of bit set to 1 in the binary representation of the integer used as an argument.

It is important to notice that the fitness function has been conceived to be smooth: an individual is rewarded even if it comes near to the number of bits set to 1 for a particular integer. The presence of a slope towards the optimum helps the evolutionary algorithm to reach the best solution.

```
#include <stdio.h>
#include <stdlib.h>
#include <math.h>
#include <stdlib.h>
#include <setjmp.h>
#include <signal.h>
#include <sys/time.h>

char           foo(char a);
```

```
static void     timeout(int);

int             bits[] = {
    0, 1, 1, 2, 1, 2, 2, 3, 1, 2, 2, 3, 2, 3, 3, 4,
    1, 2, 2, 3, 2, 3, 3, 4, 2, 3, 3, 4, 3, 4, 4, 5,
    1, 2, 2, 3, 2, 3, 3, 4, 2, 3, 3, 4, 3, 4, 4, 5,
    2, 3, 3, 4, 3, 4, 4, 5, 3, 4, 4, 5, 4, 5, 5, 6,
    1, 2, 2, 3, 2, 3, 3, 4, 2, 3, 3, 4, 3, 4, 4, 5,
    2, 3, 3, 4, 3, 4, 4, 5, 3, 4, 4, 5, 4, 5, 5, 6,
    2, 3, 3, 4, 3, 4, 4, 5, 3, 4, 4, 5, 4, 5, 5, 6,
    3, 4, 4, 5, 4, 5, 5, 6, 4, 5, 5, 6, 5, 6, 6, 7,
    1, 2, 2, 3, 2, 3, 3, 4, 2, 3, 3, 4, 3, 4, 4, 5,
    2, 3, 3, 4, 3, 4, 4, 5, 3, 4, 4, 5, 4, 5, 5, 6,
    2, 3, 3, 4, 3, 4, 4, 5, 3, 4, 4, 5, 4, 5, 5, 6,
    3, 4, 4, 5, 4, 5, 5, 6, 4, 5, 5, 6, 5, 6, 6, 7,
    2, 3, 3, 4, 3, 4, 4, 5, 3, 4, 4, 5, 4, 5, 5, 6,
    3, 4, 4, 5, 4, 5, 5, 6, 4, 5, 5, 6, 5, 6, 6, 7,
    3, 4, 4, 5, 4, 5, 5, 6, 4, 5, 5, 6, 5, 6, 6, 7,
    4, 5, 5, 6, 5, 6, 6, 7, 5, 6, 6, 7, 6, 7, 7, 8
};

static jmp_buf  wakeup_place;
static struct itimerval new;

int main(int argc, char *argv[])
{
    int         t;
    int         diff;
    float       fitness;

    if (!setjmp(wakeup_place)) {
        signal(SIGVTALRM, timeout);
        new.it_interval.tv_sec = 0;      /* next value, seconds */
        new.it_interval.tv_usec = 0;     /* next value, milliseconds */
        new.it_value.tv_sec = 0;         /* current value, seconds */
        new.it_value.tv_usec = 500;      /* current value, milliseconds */
        setitimer(ITIMER_VIRTUAL, &new, NULL);
        fitness = 0.0;
        t = 0;
    } else {
        t = 256;
    }
    while (t < 256) {
        diff = bits[t] - foo((char)t);
        if(diff > 0)
```

```
            diff = -diff;
        if (!diff) {
            fitness += 100.0;
        } else {
            fitness += exp(diff);
        }
        ++t;
    }
    printf("%f\n", fitness);

    return 0;
}


static void timeout(int foo)
{
    longjmp(wakeup_place, 1);
}
```

The C code for the `main` function that calls the assembly individuals implements also a timeout, since an individual could potentially fall into an infinite loop, given the `branchCond` macro and the fact that the initial population and subsequent mutations are randomly determined. If an individual triggers the timeout, it will have the fitness computed up to that moment. The presence of infinite loops should be always taken into account when considering code generation by evolutionary means.

12.3.3 Running

This experiment is quite complex. Depending on the hardware at your disposal, it could take hours to converge: μ and λ of the population should be dimensioned accordingly. In our experience, on a home desktop computer, it takes about 50 minutes to reach an optimal solution on 3 bits, with $\mu = 70$ and $\lambda = 35$. Finding an assembly program able to correctly evaluate all integers represented by more bits would require a bigger population and it would surely take more time.

Appendix A
Argument and option synopsis

Here is a comprehensive list of all possible options and parameters that may be used in the command line or in the settings files. It is provided as a quick reference for the user.

Only predefined keywords are reported in the table. This means that in some cases all possible values for an option or parameter are present in the table, but not all possible values for all possible options. In particular, logic value literals, numeric values, default file names do not appear as table items.

The following table has two columns. The first lists the option name, without the syntactic marks that surround it when it is used (the -- prefix on the command line, or the <option name=" and "/> tag delimiters in the settings file). The second describes where and how the option may or should be used.

The usage context indicates when the option or parameter may be used. In this field *CL* is used to indicate the command line, *SF* the settings file and *PPF* the population parameter file.

For every item that can be used in a setting file the parent is reported. A composite syntax is used to indicate the parent when it would be ambiguous to indicate just the nearest parent element. So the notation *element_1.element_2* means that the correct parent is an instance of *element_2* that appears as descendent of *element_1*. The notation *(value).element* indicates that the item can appear as a descendent of an instance of *element* enclosed in another element one of whose attribute values is *value*. This notation is unambiguous in this case because all values used in such a context only appear as attribute values of one single element. The parent is not reported if the item can only be used on the command line.

A further field reports the default value for the item. In this context *none* indicates that no default value exists and the user should provide one. The expression *not applicable* means either that the item already is a literal value, or that the item is an element with several descendents that must be present in the settings, so the concept of a default value does not make sense. If the item is a composite element that may optionally be present the default values of all its descendents are indicated in the respective fields, so the expression *see element attributes* is used.

The last field reports a brief description of the option purpose. This description is not meant for understanding its usage, only to provide a quick mnemonic reference to other parts of the book.

Table A.1: Options

Option	Description
`alterationMutation`	Usage context: PPF
	Setting type: element attribute
	Parent: `operator.ref`
	Default: *none*
	Specifies the alteration mutation operator.
`boolean`	Usage context: SF
	Setting type: attribute value
	Parent: `option.type`
	Default: *not applicable*
	Specifies that the value attribute of the enclosing element is a boolean.
`brief`	Usage context: CL, SF
	Setting type: attribute value
	Parent: `(logging).option.value`
	Default: *not applicable*
	Specifies that the logging messages should be generated in brief format, with timing information.
`cloneScalingFactor`	Usage context: PPF
	Setting type: element
	Parent: `parameters`
	Default: 0
	Multiplying factor for the fitness values of identical individuals.
`concurrentEvaluations`	Usage context: CL, PPF
	Setting type: element
	Parent: `evaluation`
	Default: 1
	Maximum number of phenotype files generated for concurrent evaluation.
`constraints`	Usage context: PPF
	Setting type: element
	Parent: `parameters`

Table A.1: Options

Option	Description
	Default: *none*
	The name of the external constraints file for the population.
`context`	Usage context: SF
	Setting type: element
	Parent: `settings`
	Default: *not applicable*
	A logically related subset of the general parameters.
`current`	Usage context: PPF
	Setting type: element attribute
	Parent: `weight`
	Default: 0
	Initial activation probability for a genetic operator.
`debug`	Usage context: CL, SF
	Setting type: attribute value
	Parent: `(logging).option.value`
	Default: *not applicable*
	Specifies that full debug messages should be sent to the standard output or to the relative logging stream.
`eliteSize`	Usage context: PPF
	Setting type: element
	Parent: `parameters`
	Default: 0
	Number of elite individuals that never age.
`enhanced`	Usage context: PPF
	Setting type: attribute value
	Parent: `parameters.type`
	Default: *not applicable*
	Specifies an enhanced population type for evolution.
`environment`	Usage context: PPF
	Setting type: element
	Parent: `parameters`
	Default: *not applicable*

Table A.1: Options

Option	Description
	The set of all environment variables used by the external evaluator.
`error`	Usage context: CL, SF
	Setting type: attribute value
	Parent: `(logging).option.value`
	Default: *not applicable*
	Specifies that only error messages should be sent to the standard output or to the relative logging stream.
`evaluation`	Usage context: PPF
	Setting type: element
	Parent: `parameters`
	Default: *none*
	The set of all parameters for evaluation.
`evaluatorInputPathName`	Usage context: CL, PPF
	Setting type: element
	Parent: `evaluation`
	Default: individual.input
	The base name of the individual phenotype, as is generated for evaluation.
`evaluatorOutputPathName`	Usage context: CL, PPF
	Setting type: element
	Parent: `evaluation`
	Default: individuals.output
	The name of the fitness file generated by the external evaluator.
`evaluatorPathName`	Usage context: CL, PPF
	Setting type: element
	Parent: `evaluation`
	Default: ./evaluator
	The name of the executable file that performs fitness evaluation.
`evolution`	Usage context: SF
	Setting type: attribute value
	Parent: `context.name`
	Default: *not applicable*

Table A.1: Options

Option	Description
	Settings for evolution related parameters.
extended	Usage context: CL, SF
	Setting type: attribute value
	Parent: (logging).option.value
	Default: *not applicable*
	Specifies that the logging messages should be generated in extended format, with all additional information.
files	Usage context: PPF
	Setting type: element
	Parent: evaluation
	Default: *none*
	Element specifying an alternative syntax for fitness evaluation parameters.
fitnessHole	Usage context: PPF
	Setting type: element attribute
	Parent: selection
	Default: *none*
	Probability of usage of a criterion alternative to fitness in tournament selection.
fitnessParameters	Usage context: PPF
	Setting type: element
	Parent: parameters
	Default: *none*
	The number of numeric fitness values produced during evaluation.
help	Usage context: CL
	Default: *not applicable*
	Causes μGP to display a summary of its command-line options or of a specific option and exit.
inertia	Usage context: PPF
	Setting type: element
	Parent: parameters
	Default: 0

Table A.1: Options

Option	Description
	Weight of the previous values of endogenous parameters in the process of self-adaptation.
`info`	Usage context: CL, SF
	Setting type: attribute value
	Parent: `(logging).option.value`
	Default: *not applicable*
	Specifies that all normal messages should be sent to the standard output or to the relative logging stream.
`input`	Usage context: PPF
	Setting type: element
	Parent: `files`
	Default: *none*
	The base name of the individual phenotype, as is generated for evaluation.
`insertionMutation`	Usage context: PPF
	Setting type: element attribute
	Parent: `operator.ref`
	Default: *none*
	Specifies the single vertex insertion mutation operator.
`integer`	Usage context: SF
	Setting type: attribute value
	Parent: `option.type`
	Default: *not applicable*
	Specifies that the value attribute of the enclosing element is an integer.
`lambda`	Usage context: PPF
	Setting type: element
	Parent: `parameters`
	Default: *none*
	The number of genetic operators applied during the reproduction phase.
`license`	Usage context: CL
	Default: *not applicable*

Table A.1: Options

Option	Description
	Causes μGP to display its license information and exit.
localScanMutation	Usage context: PPF
	Setting type: element attribute
	Parent: operator.ref
	Default: *none*
	Specifies the single parameter local scan mutation operator.
log	Usage context: CL
	Default: *not applicable*
	Allows specifying an additional logging stream.
logging	Usage context: SF
	Setting type: attribute value
	Parent: context.name
	Default: *see section 7.2*
	Settings for the logging parameters.
maximum	Usage context: PPF
	Setting type: element attribute
	Parent: weight
	Default: 0
	Maximum activation probability for a genetic operator.
maximumAge	Usage context: PPF
	Setting type: element
	Parent: parameters
	Default: *none*
	Maximum age of an individual, after which it is forcibly killed.
maximumFitness	Usage context: PPF
	Setting type: element
	Parent: parameters
	Default: *not applicable*
	Fitness value whose appearance makes evolution stop.
maximumGenerations	Usage context: PPF
	Setting type: element
	Parent: parameters
	Default: *none*

Table A.1: Options

Option	Description
	Maximum number of generations after which evolution is stopped.
`maximumSteadyStateGenerations`	Usage context: PPF
	Setting type: element
	Parent: `parameters`
	Default: *none*
	Maximum number of generations without improvements in the best fitness after which evolution is stopped.
`merge`	Usage context: CL, SF
	Setting type: attribute value
	Parent: `(evolution).option.name`
	Default: *none*
	Sequence of merge operations to perform on the populations before the evolution begins.
`minimum`	Usage context: PPF
	Setting type: element attribute
	Parent: `weight`
	Default: 0
	Minimum activation probability for a genetic operator.
`moreHelp`	Usage context: CL
	Default: *not applicable*
	Causes μGP to display help information about its internals and exit.
`mu`	Usage context: PPF
	Setting type: element
	Parent: `parameters`
	Default: *none*
	The size of the population after the survival phase.
`multiObjective`	Usage context: PPF
	Setting type: attribute value
	Parent: `parameters.type`
	Default: *not applicable*
	Specifies a multi-objective population type for evolution.
`name`	Usage context: SF, PPF

Table A.1: Options

Option	Description
	Setting type: element attribute
	Parent: *multiple*
	Default: *not applicable*
	The name attribute of a configuration element.
nu	Usage context: PPF
	Setting type: element
	Parent: parameters
	Default: *none*
	The size of the population before the first reproduction phase.
onePointSafeCrossover	Usage context: PPF
	Setting type: element attribute
	Parent: operator.ref
	Default: *none*
	Specifies the single point safe crossover operator.
onePointSafeSimpleCrossover	Usage context: PPF
	Setting type: element attribute
	Parent: operator.ref
	Default: *none*
	Specifies the single point safe simple crossover operator.
operator	Usage context: PPF
	Setting type: element
	Parent: operatorsStatistics
	Default: *not applicable*
	The set of parameters for a single genetic operator.
operatorsStatistics	Usage context: PPF
	Setting type: element
	Parent: parameters
	Default: *none*
	The set of parameters for all genetic operators.
option	Usage context: SF
	Setting type: element
	Parent: context
	Default: *not applicable*

Table A.1: Options

Option	Description
	Settings for a single general parameter.
`output`	Usage context: PPF
	Setting type: element
	Parent: `files`
	Default: *none*
	The name of the fitness file generated by the external evaluator.
`parameters`	Usage context: PPF
	Setting type: element
	Parent: none
	Default: *not applicable*
	The description of a population and all of its parameters.
`plain`	Usage context: CL, SF
	Setting type: attribute value
	Parent: `(logging).option.value`
	Default: *not applicable*
	Specifies that the logging messages should be generated in plain format, without additional information.
`population`	Usage context: CL, SF
	Setting type: element
	Parent: `(populations)`
	Default: *none*
	Description of a single population.
`populations`	Usage context: SF
	Setting type: attribute value
	Parent: `(evolution).option.name`
	Default: *see section 7.1*
	The list of populations and associated parameters files.
`randomSeed`	Usage context: CL, SF
	Setting type: attribute value
	Parent: `(evolution).option.name`
	Default: *see section 7.1*

Table A.1: Options

Option	Description
	The initial value for the random number generator.
randomWalkMutation	Usage context: PPF
	Setting type: element attribute
	Parent: operator.ref
	Default: *none*
	Specifies the single parameter random walk mutation operator.
recovery	Usage context: SF
	Setting type: attribute value
	Parent: context.name
	Default: *not applicable*
	Settings for the status recovery parameters.
recoveryDiscardFitness	Usage context: CL, SF
	Setting type: attribute value
	Parent: (recovery).option.name
	Default: true
	Determines whether fitness values are recomputed when restoring a previous run.
recoveryInput	Usage context: CL, SF
	Setting type: attribute value
	Parent: (recovery).option.name
	Default: *none*
	The name of the file from which μGP restores the current state of the run.
recoveryInputPopulations	Usage context: SF
	Setting type: attribute value
	Parent: (recovery).option.name
	Default: *none*
	The name of an additional population file to merge to the first population.
recoveryOutput	Usage context: CL, SF
	Setting type: attribute value

Table A.1: Options

Option	Description
	Parent: `(recovery).option.name`
	Default: status.xml
	The name of the file where μGP saves the current state of the run.
recoveryOverwriteOutput	Usage context: SF
	Setting type: attribute value
	Parent: `(recovery).option.name`
	Default: true
	Determines whether the status file is overwritten at every generation.
ref	Usage context: PPF
	Setting type: element attribute
	Parent: `operator`
	Default: *none*
	The name of a genetic operator.
removalMutation	Usage context: PPF
	Setting type: element attribute
	Parent: `operator.ref`
	Default: *none*
	Specifies the single vertex removal mutation operator.
removeTempFiles	Usage context: CL, PPF
	Setting type: element
	Parent: `evaluation`
	Default: true
	Determines whether phenotype files are removed after evaluation.
replacementMutation	Usage context: PPF
	Setting type: element attribute
	Parent: `operator.ref`
	Default: *none*
	Specifies the single vertex replacement mutation operator.
scanMutation	Usage context: PPF
	Setting type: element attribute
	Parent: `operator.ref`
	Default: *none*

Table A.1: Options

Option	Description
	Specifies the single parameter scan mutation operator.
`script`	Usage context: PPF
	Setting type: element
	Parent: `files`
	Default: *none*
	The name of the executable file that performs fitness evaluation.
`selection`	Usage context: PPF
	Setting type: element
	Parent: `parameters`
	Default: *see element attributes*
	The set of parameters for tournament selection.
`settings`	Usage context: SF
	Setting type: element
	Parent: none
	Default: *not applicable*
	The set of all general parameters.
`settingsFile`	Usage context: CL
	Default: ugp3.settings.xml
	The name of the settings file.
`sigma`	Usage context: PPF
	Setting type: element
	Parent: `parameters`
	Default: *none*
	Probability of repeated application of a mutation operator.
`silent`	Usage context: CL
	Default: *not applicable*
	Specifies that no messages should be sent to the standard output.
`singleParameterAlterationMutation`	Usage context: PPF
	Setting type: element attribute
	Parent: `operator.ref`
	Default: *none*
	Specifies the single parameter alteration mutation operator.
`statisticsPathName`	Usage context: CL, SF
	Setting type: attribute value

Table A.1: Options

Option	Description
	Parent: (evolution).option.name
	Default: statistics.xml
	The name of the file containing the evolutionary statistics for the run.
string	Usage context: SF
	Setting type: attribute value
	Parent: option.type
	Default: *not applicable*
	Specifies that the value attribute of the enclosing element is a string.
subGraphInsertionMutation	Usage context: PPF
	Setting type: element attribute
	Parent: operator.ref
	Default: *none*
	Specifies the single subgraph insertion mutation operator.
subGraphRemovalMutation	Usage context: PPF
	Setting type: element attribute
	Parent: operator.ref
	Default: *none*
	Specifies the single subgraph removal mutation operator.
subGraphReplacementMutation	Usage context: PPF
	Setting type: element attribute
	Parent: operator.ref
	Default: *none*
	Specifies the single subgraph replacement mutation operator.
tau	Usage context: PPF
	Setting type: element attribute
	Parent: selection
	Default: 1
	Initial size of tournament selection.
tauMax	Usage context: PPF
	Setting type: element attribute
	Parent: selection
	Default: 1

Table A.1: Options

Option	Description
	Maximum size of tournament selection.
tauMin	Usage context: PPF
	Setting type: element attribute
	Parent: selection
	Default: 1
	Minimum size of tournament selection.
tournament	Usage context: PPF
	Setting type: attribute value
	Parent: selection.type
	Default: *none*
	Specifies regular tournament selection.
tournamentWithFitnessHole	Usage context: PPF
	Setting type: attribute value
	Parent: selection.type
	Default: *none*
	Specifies tournament selection with a fitness hole.
twoPointSafeSimpleCrossover	Usage context: PPF
	Setting type: element attribute
	Parent: operator.ref
	Default: *none*
	Specifies the two point safe simple crossover operator.
type	Usage context: SF, PPF
	Setting type: element attribute
	Parent: *multiple*
	Default: *not applicable*
	The type attribute of a configuration element.
value	Usage context: SF, PPF
	Setting type: element attribute
	Parent: *multiple*
	Default: *not applicable*
	The value attribute of a configuration element.
variable	Usage context: PPF
	Setting type: element
	Parent: environment

Table A.1: Options

Option	Description
	Default: *none*
	Name and value of a single environment variable.
`verbose`	Usage context: CL, SF
	Setting type: attribute value
	Parent: `(logging).option.value`
	Default: *not applicable*
	Specifies that verbose messages should be sent to the standard output or to the relative logging stream.
`version`	Usage context: CL
	Default: *not applicable*
	Causes μGP to display its version information and exit.
`warning`	Usage context: CL, SF
	Setting type: attribute value
	Parent: `(logging).option.value`
	Default: *not applicable*
	Specifies that only error and warning messages should be sent to the standard output or to the relative logging stream.
`weight`	Usage context: PPF
	Setting type: element
	Parent: `operator`
	Default: *see element attributes*
	The activation probablities for a single genetic operator.
`xml`	Usage context: CL, SF
	Setting type: attribute value
	Parent: `(logging).option.value`
	Default: *not applicable*
	Specifies that the logging messages should be generated in XML format, with full information.

Appendix B
External constraints synopsis

In the following is a complete list of all possible options and parameters that may be used in the external constraints files. It is provided as a quick reference for the user.

The format of the table and the reported fields are as in appendix A, with two important differences. The first one is that all items in this table refer to the external constraints, therefore the usage context does not appear in the table. The second is that, since μGP has no knowledge of the problem domain, no default value is defined for most items. The default is only reported when it exists.

Table B.1: Constraints

Constraint	Description
`averageOccurs`	Setting type: element attribute
	Parent: `macros`
	The average number of vertices corresponding to macros of the subsection in an individual.
`base`	Setting type: element attribute
	Parent: `item(bitArray)`
	Specifies that the parameter should be expressed in a particular base.
`bin`	Setting type: attribute value
	Parent: `item(bitArray).base`
	Specifies binary representation for a bit array parameter.
`bitArray`	Setting type: attribute value
	Parent: `item.xsi:type`
	Specifies a parameter composed by an array of bits.
`commentFormat`	Setting type: element
	Parent: `constraints`

Table B.1: Constraints

Constraint	Description
	The expression for the format of comments in the phenotype.
`constant`	Setting type: attribute value
	Parent: `item.xsi:type`
	Specifies a parameter whose value is one of a set of constants.
`constraints`	Setting type: element
	Parent: *none*
	Descriptions of all the constraints.
`definedType`	Setting type: attribute value
	Parent: `item.xsi:type`
	Specifies a parameter of a type previously defined by the user.
`environment`	Setting type: attribute value
	Parent: `item.xsi:type`
	Specifies a parameter whose value is that of an environment variable.
`epilogue`	Setting type: element
	Parent: *multiple*
	Epilogue for a phenotype, section or subsection.
`epilogue`	Setting type: element attribute
	Parent: *multiple*
	Specifies whether the parameter can refer to the subgraph epilogue.
`expand`	Setting type: element attribute
	Parent: `subSection`
	Specifies whether a subgraph can be shared by different references.
	Default: `false`
`expression`	Setting type: element
	Parent: *multiple*
	The phenotype expression for a macro, a prologue or an epilogue.
`float`	Setting type: attribute value
	Parent: `item.xsi:type`
	Specifies a floating point parameter.
`hex`	Setting type: attribute value
	Parent: `item(bitArray).base`

Table B.1: Constraints

Constraint	Description
	Specifies hexadecimal representation for a bit array parameter.
`id`	Setting type: element attribute
	Parent: *multiple*
	The identifier of an element in the constraints.
`identifierFormat`	Setting type: element
	Parent: `constraints`
	The expression for the format of identifiers in the phenotype.
`infinity`	Setting type: attribute value
	Parent: *multiple*
	Specifies that the entity corresponding to the containing element may occur an unlimited number of times in the individual.
`innerBackwardLabel`	Setting type: attribute value
	Parent: `item.xsi:type`
	Specifies a structural parameter that references a vertex in the same subgraph, non strictly preceding the vertex to which it belongs.
`innerForwardLabel`	Setting type: attribute value
	Parent: `item.xsi:type`
	Specifies a structural parameter that references a vertex in the same subgraph, non strictly folowing the vertex to which it belongs.
`innerGenericLabel`	Setting type: attribute value
	Parent: `item.xsi:type`
	Specifies a structural parameter that references a vertex in the same subgraph.
`integer`	Setting type: attribute value
	Parent: `item.xsi:type`
	Specifies an integer parameter.
`item`	Setting type: element
	Parent: *multiple*

Table B.1: Constraints

Constraint	Description
	A single item in a type or parameter definition.
`itself`	Setting type: element attribute
	Parent: *multiple*
	Specifies whether the parameter can refer to same vertex to which it belongs.
`labelFormat`	Setting type: element
	Parent: `constraints`
	The expression for the format of labels in the phenotype.
`length`	Setting type: element attribute
	Parent: `item(bitArray)`
	The number of bits in the parameter.
`macro`	Setting type: element
	Parent: `macros`
	A single macro in a subsection.
`macros`	Setting type: element
	Parent: `subSection`
	The set of all macros in a subsection.
`maximum`	Setting type: element attribute
	Parent: *multiple*
	The maximum value of the parameter.
`maxOccurs`	Setting type: element attribute
	Parent: *multiple*
	The minimum number of subgraphs or vertices corresponing to the parent element that can exist in an individual.
`maxReferences`	Setting type: element attribute
	Parent: `subSection`
	The maximum number of references to the prologue of the subsection in an individual.
`minimum`	Setting type: element attribute
	Parent: *multiple*
	The minimum value of the parameter.

Table B.1: Constraints

Constraint	Description
minOccurs	Setting type: element attribute
	Parent: *multiple*
	The minimum number of subgraphs or vertices corresponding to the parent element that can exist in an individual.
name	Setting type: element attribute
	Parent: item
	The name of a parameter definition or of a type definition.
oct	Setting type: attribute value
	Parent: item(bitArray).base
	Specifies octal representation for a bit array parameter.
outerLabel	Setting type: attribute value
	Parent: item.xsi:type
	Specifies a structural parameter that references the prologue of a different subgraph.
param	Setting type: element
	Parent: macro
	A parameter in the expression of a macro, prologue or epilogue.
parameters	Setting type: element
	Parent: *multiple*
	The set of parameters that appear in a prologue, epilogue or macro expression.
pattern	Setting type: element attribute
	Parent: item(bitArray)
	Specifies value constraints in the parameter.
prologue	Setting type: element
	Parent: *multiple*
	Prologue for a phenotype, section or subsection.
prologue	Setting type: element attribute
	Parent: *multiple*
	Specifies whether the parameter can refer to the subgraph prologue.

Table B.1: Constraints

Constraint	Description
`prologueEpilogueCompulsory`	Setting type: element attribute
	Parent: `section`
	Specifies whether the prologue and epilogue of a section should always exist in the phenotype.
`ref`	Setting type: element
	Parent: `item(outerLabel)`
	The reference of a structural parameter to a subgraph type.
`ref`	Setting type: element attribute
	Parent: *multiple*
	A reference of a parameter to a parameter definition, or of a parameter definition to a type definition.
`section`	Setting type: element
	Parent: `sections`
	A single section in the constraints.
`section`	Setting type: element attribute
	Parent: `item(outerLabel).ref`
	The section in the constraints containing the subsection to which the target subgraph corresponds.
`sections`	Setting type: element
	Parent: `constraints`
	The set of all sections in the constraints.
`selfRef`	Setting type: attribute value
	Parent: `item.xsi:type`
	Specifies a structural parameter that references the vertex to which it belongs.
`sigma`	Setting type: element attribute
	Parent: `macros`
	The standard deviation in the number of vertices corresponding to macros of the subsection in the individuals composing the initial population.
`subSection`	Setting type: element
	Parent: `subSections`
	A single subsection in a section.

Table B.1: Constraints

Constraint	Description
subSection	Setting type: element attribute
	Parent: `item(outerLabel).ref`
	The subsection in the constraints to which the target subgraph corresponds.
subSections	Setting type: element
	Parent: `section`
	The set of all subsections in a section.
typeDefinitions	Setting type: element
	Parent: `constraints`
	The set of type definitions for use in the phenotype expressions.
uniqueTag	Setting type: attribute value
	Parent: `item.xsi:type`
	Specifies a parameter that expands to a unique symbol.
uniqueTagFormat	Setting type: element
	Parent: `constraints`
	The expression for the format of unique tags in the phenotype.
value	Setting type: element
	Parent: *multiple*
	Declarator of a literal value or placeholder for an actual value.
variable	Setting type: element attribute
	Parent: `item(environment)`
	The name of the environment variable whose value is assigned to the parameter.
weight	Setting type: element attribute
	Parent: `macro`
	A non-normalized indication of the probability of occurrence of vertices corresponding to the enclosing macro in a random individual.
	Default: 1.0
xsi:schemaLocation	Setting type: element attribute
	Parent: `constraints`

Table B.1: Constraints

Constraint	Description
	URL of the schema for the constraints document type.
`xsi:type`	Setting type: element attribute
	Parent: `item`
	The name of a parameter type.
`xmlns`	Setting type: element attribute
	Parent: `constraints`
	The XML namespace of the constraints document type.
`xmlns:xsi`	Setting type: element attribute
	Parent: `constraints`
	XML schema instance for the constraints document type.

References

1. G. E. P. Box. Evolutionary operation: A method for increasing industrial prouctivity. *Applied Statistics*, VI, no. 2:81–101, 1957.
2. H. J. Bremermann. *Optimization through Evolution and Recombination*. Spartan Books, 1962.
3. W. D. Cannon. *The Wisdom of the body*. W.W.Norton, 1932.
4. C. Darwin. *On the Origin of Species by Means of Natural Selection, or the Preservation of Favoured Races in the Struggle for Life*. Murray, London, 1859.
5. R. Dawkins. *The Selfish Gene*. Oxford University Press, 1982.
6. David B. Fogel. *Evolutionary computation: toward a new philosophy of machine intelligence*. IEEE Press, Piscataway, NJ, USA, 1995.
7. L. J. Fogel. Autonomous automata. *Industrial Research*, 4:14–19, 1962.
8. L. J. Fogel. Toward inductive inference automata. In *Proceeding of the International Federation for Information Processing Congress*, pages 395–400, 1962.
9. A. S. Frazer. Simulation of genetic systems by automatic digital computers (part 1). *Australian Journal of Biological Science*, 10:484–491, 1957.
10. A. S. Frazer. Simulation of genetic systems by automatic digital computers (part 1). *Australian Journal of Biological Science*, 10:492–499, 1957.
11. R. M. Friedberg. A learning machine: Part i. *IBM Journal*, 2(1):2–13, 1958.
12. S. J. Gould. *The Dinosaur in the Haystack*. Harmony Books, 1995.
13. H.-P.Schwefel. *Cybernetic Evolution as Strategy for Experimental Research in Fluid Mechanics (Diploma Thesis in German)*. Hermann Fttinger-Institute for Fluid Mechanics, Technical University of Berlin, 1965.
14. J. H. Holland. *Adaptation in Natural and Artificial Systems: An Introductory Analysis with Applications to Biology, Control and Artificial Intelligence*. The University of Michigan Press, 1975.
15. E. W. Mayr. *Toward a new Philosophy of Biological Thought: Diversity, Evolution and Inheritance*. Belknap, Harvard, 1982.
16. R. M. Friedberg; B. Dunham; J. H. North. A learning machine: Part ii. *IBM Journal*, 3(7):282–287, 1959.
17. I. Rechenberg. *Evolutionsstrategie - Optimierung technischer Systeme nach Prinzipien der biologischen Evolution (PhD thesis)*. (Reprinted by) Fromman-Holzboog, 1971.
18. Lee Smolin. *The Life of the Cosmos*. Weidenfeld and Nicolson, London, 1997.
19. F. Corno; M. Sonza Reorda; G. Squillero. Exploiting the selfish gene algorithm for evolving cellular automata. *Neural Networks, 2000. IJCNN 2000, Proceedings of the IEEE-INNS-ENNS International Joint Conference on*, 6:577–581 vol.6, 2000.
20. A. M. Turing. Computing machinery and intelligence. *Mind*, 9:433–360, 1950.
21. C. Darwin; A. R. Wallace. On the tendency of species to form varieties; and on the perpetuation of varieties and species by natural means of selection. *Journal of the Proceedings of the Linnean Society of London*, Zoology 3:46–50, 1858.

22. Franz Weiling. Historical study: Johann gregor mendel 18221884. *American Journal of Medical Genetics*, 40(26):1–25, 1991.
23. August Weismann. *Evolution Theory*. Arnold, London, 1904.
24. Wojciech Hubert Zurek. Decoherence, einselection, and the quantum origins of the classical. *Reviews of Modern Physics*, 75, 2003.